Working Dad

How To Win In Your Career and Fatherhood

Farhan Qureshi

Published by Working Parent 2013

Working Parent is a division of Digitopia Studios Ltd.

Copyright © Farhan Qureshi 2013

ISBN 978 0 9927340 0 8

Farhan Qureshi has asserted his right under the Copyright, Designs and Patent Act 1988 to be identified as the author of this work.

Disclaimer:
This book contains information from many years of research and practical experience, whilst this has been successful for the author, no guarantees are made that the same results will apply to the reader. Advice and knowledge in here must be tailored to the reader's individual circumstances.

Everything in this book is

by dads, for dads.

About the Author

First and foremost, Farhan is a dad of two from London, in the UK. Much like you, he's a working dad. For the day job, he is a filmmaker and VFX artist, and has worked on such movies as *Harry Potter 3, 4* and *5, Batman Begins, Poseidon, Alien vs Predator, Riddick* and *The Pirates! in an Adventure with Scientists* (UK title)/*Band of Misfits* (US title).

Working long hours and travelling frequently for business, Farhan is passionate in helping working parents maximise the quality of time they have with their children. This book is the result of much research with working parents, and aims to help fathers balance the many demands of sustaining a thriving career alongside raising a happy family while always following your passion and achieving your dreams.

Farhan runs the website www.workingParent.info, a forum where working parents can support one another and share stories, tips and advice on balancing work, raising children and making time for themselves. Farhan has also written the number 1 bestselling book *VFX and CG Survival Guide for Producers and Filmmakers*. Farhan also runs the popular filmmakers and VFX artists website www.digitopiaFilm.com.

About the Editor

Vicki Watson is a writer, editor and book designer whose publications have ranged from business books, teacher resource guides and parental handbooks to children's workbooks, fiction and poetry. Her latest book is *Bob and the Alien Escapade*, a sci-fi adventure book for 7-12 year-olds. After a career as a teacher and deputy headteacher, she decided to focus on her love of language and design and set up Callisto Green, a vibrant and dynamic writing and design venture and small publishing imprint where she now spends her days playing with words and pictures.

When she's not scribbling in her notebook, her many interests include playing the clarinet, rock-climbing, stargazing and playing chess. She lives in Wiltshire with her husband and three sons.

You can find out more about Vicki or contact her through her website at www.callistogreen.com.

Start here…

This book is for you. Yes, you. You the dad. This book isn't about how to get a baby to sleep through the night or how to potty train a toddler. This book isn't about raising children or how to send them to Oxford, Cambridge, Yale or Harvard. This book is entirely, one hundred percent for you, you the dad or the dad-to-be.

Everything in this book is by dads, for dads.

Contents

Author's Note

We've all see pictures similar to this one. I went through a period of travelling away for work pretty much every single week. What this picture says became a big part of my parenting philosphy and in part inspired me to write this book. A lot of the book is based upon the message behind this picture.

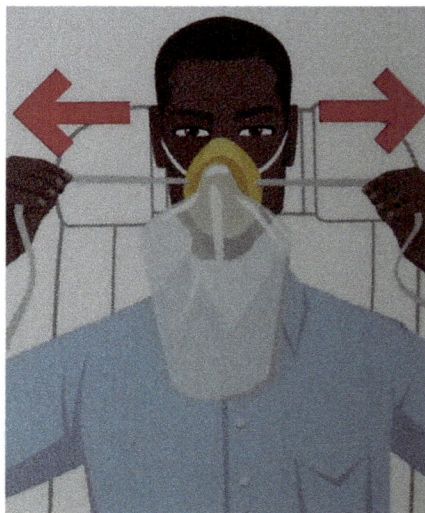

I've spent four years putting this book together as I believe there is more to parenting than sacrifice and you as a dad have the right to give yourself and your dreams some priority too.

Preface

I am writing this section on a flight from London to Montreal. You see, in order to be a super-dad, as well as spending time with your kids, you sometimes have to be away from them and earn the cash, whether it's Pounds, Dollars, Euros, Rupees, Yen, wherever you're from, all languages speak money.

I did all my packing when my two boys (the elder three years old and the youngest just six weeks) were asleep. I had a few hours' sleep, took them swimming in the morning and then rushed like a maniac to the airport to catch my flight. Now I'm going to be away from them for several months. By the time I next see my youngest boy, he will have spent over half his life away from me – nobody said being a dad was easy.

In this book we'll look together at our role in this game of child raising, what do we do when we are away from our kids, and whether it's possible to be good fathers when we are away so often?

Ultimately, when we are away from home, it is for one reason – to earn money. But how much is this money worth compared to the time we are missing in seeing our children grow up? Get ready to see how it's possible to have both, to earn more money than ever and still have plenty of time to spend with your children.

To my dad for teaching me what it means to be a real dad.

To Zak and Adam, for making me follow through on those lessons.

Introduction

So you're a high flyer, a ladder-climber, on your way to the top and then, bang, your partner gets pregnant! Suddenly, you're going to be a dad. Or maybe it's the other way around – you've already got children and now you're realising that you need to be higher up on that career path.

Whichever way around the story goes, make no mistake about it: being a dad is a challenging proposition, made even more so today by increased demands and societal expectations. That's not to discount the work of dads over the past generations; indeed, they did a sterling job. But dads today have different challenges than the dads of yesteryear. These challenges can be thought of in two parts – economic and domestic. Some of the economic challenges include the facts that:

- There are no jobs for life anymore, and gone are the days when the first job you had was your only job. Today, the average male worker can expect to change jobs and careers a dozen or so times before they hit retirement. And that's if they hit retirement at all.

- Final salary pensions are fast becoming a rarity.

- House prices are higher multiples of the average salary than ever, so a mortgage at four times your basic salary is a thing of the past.

- An increasingly global work environment means that employers, from large corporations to small companies, all have access to a wider and cheaper workforce. If it hasn't happened already, your job could be outsourced for a tenth of your day rate to someone in another part of the world.

Due to the changing role of women the modern dad has expectations placed upon him that differ from those his father and grandfather experienced. Whilst having the same physical traits as their 1960s counterparts, today's women are very different to how their mothers and grandmothers were at an equivalent age. Of course, this is a good thing, a positive move to greater equality and well overdue. But as well as carrying out all those other roles that previous generations of fathers fulfilled, you, my friend, now have a whole host of other responsibilities and tasks that previous generations did not have. Things like changing nappies, sharing household chores and spending time with your children – and yes, you've still got to find enough money to buy that house that's currently on the market for ten times your annual salary.

If this sounds like a gloomy book, a portent of the end of the world, fret not, this book is written for you, and will help you to juggle the demands placed upon you and thrive at work and at home. Over the following chapters, we are going to look at how you can:

Enjoy overcoming these challenges (yes, I did say enjoy!).

- Get ahead of the pack.

- Have enough time to spend with your children.

- Most importantly, have enough time and energy for yourself and the things that you like doing – remember those things you used to do for fun before you became a dad?

Take off – you thought your career was going well before you had kids

Remember your single and free days, when you were the go-getter, when you were the rising star in the office and when you scoffed at that middle manager in his thirties with two kids, struggling with mortgage repayments and owning the crappiest car in the car park? It's okay, we all did it. And remember how you promised yourself that you'd never be that tubby, bespectacled, balding, stressed-out guy? Remember feeling confident that you'd never have a receding hairline or a bulging waistline?

You might have even promised yourself that you would never be pressured into missing your child's birthday, that you'd stand up to your boss and that you'd never put a deadline ahead of a weekend with your family.

Well, have a look around yourself now.

Can you see those whizz-kids looking at you? They're still young, free and single, and yes, they're probably looking at you today and promising themselves that they'll handle it better than you currently are.

It's not that I'm making any inferences to your hairline, or even waistline for that matter, but we all know that the pressures we face today mean that we are taking shortcuts. Shortcuts with our health, with our diet and increasingly with our relationships. This book is going to focus on those relationships and on making sure that whatever else may be receding in our lives, that our relationships with our kids and partner/wife/girlfriend (I'm going to use the terms interchangeably) will never be one of those, in fact our relationship with our family will flourish.

NOTE: A very quick word about 'his/her', 'pounds/dollars/euros etc.', 'wife/girlfriend/partner/significant-other' constructs. I am going to use these terms interchangeably to avoid blunders. If I use the word 'his', it could equally apply to her, if I use the word 'pound', it could equally mean 'dollar', 'euro', 'rupee', 'dirham', 'bhatt' and so on. 'Wife' could also apply to 'girlfriend', although we'll assume you have one or the other! Lastly, when I say 'Dad' I actually mean 'breadwinner'; all of these lessons could apply to mothers as well, it's simply that The Working Mum/Dad Guide or The Good Breadwinner Guide doesn't have the same ring to it and there's no Amazon category for breadwinner at the time of publishing.

Meet your new boss

Whether your kid is on her way or is already here, the fact is that amongst the many things that are about to be turned on their heads, you are also about to get a new boss. In fact, you're going to find yourself falling down the pecking line quite a lot. Your partner and your child will become or already are now your main concerns and they each have their own rights and requirements from you. Maybe your partner was quite independent and not especially reliant upon you before, but during pregnancy and the initial weeks after the birth, you are going to need to attend to her around the clock. And of course the new baby is also going to be constantly requiring attention. So two new bosses at least, and more for multiple births.

But what about your existing boss? You know, the one at the office?

You still have a job to go to, your work still needs to be done and you still need to earn money. We'll talk more about whether you can really afford to take two weeks paternity leave in the upcoming chapters; this chapter is about having enough time and energy to satisfy the requirements of all your bosses.

Work may suddenly seem meaningless and trivial when compared to the childbearing and childrearing process. But work is what puts money into your bank account, food on the table and a roof over your heads. With an extra person to support, coupled with the potential loss of one of the household incomes, you are now more than ever going to have to make sure you stay on the right side of your boss.

This is how your situation is going to change:

i. You are going to be massively sleep-deprived – please do not underestimate the effects of this. You are going to be massively distracted from your day job.

ii. Your new situation needs plenty of time to get used to – you will be constantly adjusting your routine as your child goes through different stages of development.

iii. You will start to meet other new parents who earn more money than you – whether you deny it or not, there is going to be pressure to keep up with these new parents. It may be direct, but is more likely to be indirect and insidious.

iv. Your work colleagues will not be going through the same problems that you are. Depending upon how ruthless your office environment is, these guys may even push harder to exploit your weaknesses. It's a dog-eat-dog world out there and you know what happens when dogs smell fear.

Whilst every work situation is different, they all hold true to the same premise, which is, if you start failing at work you will be replaced, no ifs, no buts, no maybes.

Of course, this is true of any time, but in this economic turmoil that we are living in, you really don't want to find out if you can fail twice. Unfortunately, the opposite isn't necessarily true; as much as we like to believe that the better we do, the better we will be rewarded, society sadly doesn't always follow a meritocracy. Regardless of the rights or wrongs of it, you now need to be earning more money than you did before.

Unless you start early, you will be fighting an uphill struggle. The costs of nappies, bottles and furniture are just the beginning. You will find that after becoming a parent, you'll start to notice things that you didn't notice before, especially around the neighbourhood you live in. Suddenly you'll start to see it for what it really is and wonder if this is really the kind of place you want your kids to grow up in. You may have ambitions of sending them to a private school, upgrading your car or going on exotic holidays, but all of these things require a lot of capital. Even more reason why focusing on your work and keeping your boss happy are now more important than before.

Get to work on time, no matter what

Your partner may suffer from being less mobile than normal for some degree of time, so she'll probably need your time and help in the mornings before you leave for work. It may be the only chance in the day that she gets to have a shower or grab something to eat. Whilst it's noble that you're giving her that break in the morning, it is imperative that you also get yourself to work on time. Your boss doesn't care that you sterilised all the bottles and gave the baby a bath before work. I'm going to repeat that because it's really important that you understand this: *Your boss does not care that you sterilised all the bottles and gave the baby a bath before work.* But your boss does care that you get to work on time and do your job. After all, he has his own concerns and his own bosses, who in turn care even less about sterilised bottles and baby baths.

So how are you supposed to say no to a new mother who asks if you could take the new-born for ten minutes?

Well in reality, you can't say no.

But you can get yourself ready beforehand and make sure you are all set to go before you are called into action. You can pre-empt a lot of the to-do tasks before you are asked to do them, like preparing all the bottles and clothes before you go to bed the night before. The idea is that everything you need to start the following day should be ready the previous evening, leaving no tasks for the morning, not least because babies are unpredictable. They may not sleep through the night or they may get up an hour earlier than expected. The point is that you just do not know what your baby will throw at you, and you don't want to start the day chasing your tail.

Agree on a time when you need to leave for work and make sure you hit that time. In the grand scheme of things, the money that you bring back is more important than changing that extra nappy or putting away the dishes. And it's not enough that you understand this – you need to make sure that your partner understands it too (although in all fairness, she probably understands it better than you do).

Try to avoid falling into the male guilt trap that many new fathers do. 'Male guilt' is a term I invented; it refers to the fact that some new fathers feel guilty for putting their wives through the pains of pregnancy, the agony of childbirth and the subsequent postnatal side effects. Yes, she has been through a lot – a hell of a lot more than you have – but feeling guilty for putting her through that is counterproductive.

So of course you want to help as much as you can. In an ideal world, you'd get up, get yourself ready before she and the baby wake up and then do whatever needs to be done around the house. And you'd still get to work on time. In reality, though, that can be a pretty tall order every day, so stop feeling guilty and focus on what you can do, not on what you can't or didn't. Beating yourself up over things is counterproductive and won't help either her or yourself.

At the office

Now that you've arrived on time, it's important to focus on the job and not get distracted by your mental to-do list. One strategy is to throw yourself into your work like never before. You may not be able to stay as late as the rest of the team, or for as long as you were accustomed to before, so you now need to increase your efficiency and work smarter than any of your colleagues. Set yourself targets well ahead of any deliveries you may have, so that you'll have a buffer zone for when you've got to field unexpected calls from your partner (sadly, she's less likely to be whispering sweet-nothings down the phone, and more likely to be calling with a list of things you need to bring or do on your way home – if she mentions the bedroom, it will be in terms of repairs you'll be making to the room!). The further ahead of schedule you can be, the more time you can give to these extra tasks.

If you want to succeed at work, you are going to have to become much more visible than before. Whereas previously you may have got on with your work quietly and without making a fuss, now you will need to check with your schedule/workload to track your progress more. I'm not saying to make a big song and dance whenever you are doing well, but to just try to be a little more visible. This strategy works equally for when you are ahead and for when you are behind, for example, when you need additional resources or time. All being well, your employer will see you making an extra effort and delivering in advance of your milestones, which will help you on your next quest: getting ahead of the game. Your boss may well be sympathetic to your new situation, but don't expect any special treatment. You are not the first person in the world to have a child and hold down a full-time job. There is probably a whole collection of other dads in the office and they can't all get special treatment. You've had your paternity leave, so now get on with it.

Attack it in two ways: first survive then pull away from the pack

The biggest obstacle to your survival is the sleep deprivation that you are going to suffer. It will happen and it'll vary from night to night. Ideally, try to get the baby into a routine as soon as possible. Reading through the numerous baby-raising books (of which this book is not one), it may seem that getting your baby into a routine is a bit cruel and unintuitive. It's true the methods that some of these books use to get a baby into routine could be considered to be cruel, but you will see parents following these routine pattern-building plans with military-style precision. This may not be you (it certainly wasn't me) but there are plenty of upsides to getting your child into an early routine (as well as some downsides in terms of not being able to go out and enjoy your time with your child because it could spoil the routine). The point here is to investigate it fully yourself. From what I have seen, the primary reason to get your child into a routine is for you, the parent, to have more time for yourself. Controversial, maybe; selfish, yes. But you're not being selfish so that you can spend more time watching sports (although you will have time to watch sports) – you're doing it so that you can have more energy and time to earn more money and in consequence have more 'quality' time to spend with your kids.

Until this occurs, consider stealing time to have a powernap. Even ten minutes' snooze during your lunch hour can charge you up for the rest of the day. Maybe there's a library nearby (the reference section is an excellent place), where you'll find lots of other people power-napping away. The train is good too, although be careful not to miss your stop! Don't be surprised to find a secret society of snoozers in places of worship or quiet reflection. You need to maintain your energy levels and perform well at work, and sleep gives you the best energy.

Despite the need to earn more money to afford the things you want for your family, one of the things you can afford to spend on is good quality food and drink for yourself whilst you are struggling with sleep deprivation – so go ahead and buy that freshly squeezed orange juice at the station. You are going to gain more in health benefits than you will lose by saving a few pounds.

How to survive your paternity leave

Two weeks off work, paid to spend time with your partner and new-born, may sound like a free holiday, but it's not. At first, you'll be very excited and anticipate that the fortnight of paternity leave will be a breeze. But if you don't manage this time properly, you'll find it a long, drawn-out affair, leaving you screaming to be allowed back to work as quickly as possible.

So how to make those two weeks more of a blissful retreat with your new family and less like house arrest?

Firstly, create a plan. It doesn't have to be super-precise, but you should know what's expected of you and when. A bit of forward planning will prevent you from feeling overworked and underappreciated. Much like your office work doesn't stop when you have a baby, neither will your housework stop. Laundry will still need to done, carpets vacuumed, dishes cleaned, beds made and so on. This is not a fairy tale. The clothes won't wash themselves and the floors won't become magically sparkling at the click of a finger. Read through the baby books about all the things that you will require and act upon them ahead of time; you really don't want to be still assembling your new-born's cot when the baby is crying to go in there.

I'm not going to dwell on the practicalities of the endless to-do list – that's not the aim of book. Instead, I am going to talk about you, how during this period of newfound home bliss, you are going to be neglected and pushed to the background and how best to deal with these feelings of sudden invisibility. Goodness knows when your child

11

is born and your partner is recovering, no one is going to be asking how you are coping. Even to your friends and family, you are going to appear to be a bit part player who isn't doing much to merit any attention.

Yet really, the opposite is true. Whilst you may not have performed the most difficult tasks of giving birth and being born, you are still doing something. Not everything, admittedly, but you're playing a vital part in the proceedings. Even if no one else acknowledges this part, it's important that you recognise your role and believe that what you are doing is important. If you don't, you will spend your two weeks of paternity leave feeling underappreciated and undervalued. It's a thankless task and people will only notice when the house isn't clean or when something isn't done – welcome to the world of the housewife/househusband. Preparing yourself for this will not prevent it happening, but it will cushion the blow for you when it does.

4

Double trouble – when you have more than one child

When you have your second child, you as a father are naturally going to be spending more time with the older child as the new-born is more dependent upon her mother. But whilst you and the older child will be having fun going on play dates, you still want to spend time with the newborn and your partner.

There is a wealth of material on how to introduce the older child to their new sibling, how to avoid jealousy, how they will react to each other and how to let them know that they are loved equally. Yet almost nothing has been written about you and how you are going to be dropping down the pecking order even further.

Go back to the time where you were number one with your partner. She adored you for a number of reasons, none of which included you keeping the household ticking over financially. Certainly for the first couple of years of parenthood, it is unrealistic to expect to be your partner's number one priority like before, but that is not to say that you cannot rekindle those early heady days.

Know that you are more than just the financier of this project. Act like a good father and make yourself indispensable with the kids and they'll put you as number one. Spending time with them doing fun things that you all enjoy doing will make your kids gravitate to you. Put down your work and your chores whilst the kids are awake and pick them back up again when they are asleep. In fact, go as far as turning off your Wi-Fi and phone whilst you are spending time with your children.

The astute amongst you will realise that the more chores you are doing whilst the kids are sleeping, the less time you are going to have for yourself and for doing the things that you want to do. In subsequent chapters, we are going to discuss how to do things faster and be more discerning about what things actually need doing. For now I want to keep on the track of how you are going to cope with the neglect that you may feel.

First, recognise that your feelings are important and that they do count too. Your girlfriend may not have time to field your emotions right now; it's understandable, given what she has been through. But know that it is temporary. If you know she cannot give you the attention that you need, then find someone who you are able to talk to, someone who doesn't necessarily know her and ideally someone who isn't that interested in babies.

Make time to celebrate the birth of your new child with your friends. You are going to experience a change in your friendships and with whom you associate. And you may find yourself still yearning for that carefree life of reckless abandon before you had all these responsibilities. But chances are, that will start to wear thin. It's going to take time for you to adjust to your new circumstances and status and the shift between non-dad and dad that you're going through is huge. Your non-dad and single friends are going to notice it too, and your relationship with them and their attitudes towards you are going to shift. You'll start developing new interests and making friends with people whom you now have more in common with, i.e. new dads like yourself. Even though the majority of your conversations will be centred around your new child, having these discussions with other new dads and sharing your experiences are important. Even though you may be strangers, you will be able to express yourself to them and forming a group where you are valued as a father and not judged because you didn't do as much as your partner.

Some playgroups run dad's time (although some of them call it dads time). Make use of this; you will be surprised at just how much you'll enjoy having sole responsibility for your child in an external environment. There are also a plethora of classes that you can take your child to at the weekends. Most of the sports classes are filled with fathers and their kids. Though it's not advertised as an official dad's time, you'll notice that it's a time when working fathers can spend time with their kids doing what they (the dads) want to do. This is probably better than a dad's time organised by a nursery, since you choose the activity that you enjoy, rather than what a nursery worker thinks you 'should' enjoy. Also, you will be able to meet and talk with other fathers who enjoy the same activity as you. As well as being about the sport/activity, it is also a mutual admiration society where fathers all knowingly appreciate both their own and the other fathers' contributions.

Taking your child to baby and toddler groups during the week is also a good way to meet other parents. Generally these groups will be mainly mothers, so don't be surprised to find yourself the only father present. But therein is an opportunity, as these mothers are generally supportive and want to hear your experiences. Just because your own partner may not be keen to hear about your struggles over hers, don't think mothers in general aren't interested; they are, as are the staff in these places.

Certainly they're likely to be more receptive to hearing your concerns than you would imagine, and because they've been there too, they provide an outlet for you to speak realistically about your experiences, in a way that your single/non-dad friends won't be able to match. But regardless of who you're speaking to, do try to take a break from talking about your kids every now and again and relive the life you had before fatherhood. Getting it out of your system will help keep you centred and be a better father when you are with your children.

5

Trading your time for money

No matter how much you love your job, the bottom line is that you are trading your time for money. That means time away from your kids, and no amount of money is worth more than those cherished moments with your children. This chapter is about maximising the ratio between spending time away from your children and the amount of money you can earn from that time.

So how can you optimally trade your time for the maximum amount of money? It depends upon a number of different factors:

- What job do you do?

- What skills do you have?

- What level of relevant education and experience do you have?

- What is the demand for your skills?

- How much time do you spend travelling/commuting to work?

Some of the answers to these questions are related to your past. You can't change your past – the past belongs to yesterday, today belongs to you and tomorrow depends upon what you choose to do with today. But the past can teach you lessons.

Everything about your life – your home, your job, your partner, your body – is the result of the choices and decisions you have made or not made. If a man chooses to eat ten cakes every day of his life, smoke five packets of cigarettes a day and drink until he has no money left, after ten years, that man is going to be a fat b&st&rd with a heart condition and no money – it's not an accident and he needn't be surprised when he doesn't fit into those jeans he purchased when he was twenty. Note the use of the word 'choose'; everything is your choice, simple cause and effect.

There is a reason that some people earn a lot of money and others don't. It has nothing to do with where you are from, what opportunities you've had, the colour of your skin, which school you went to or whether you grew up on a council estate or in a posh, leafy suburb. People who believe these factors have anything to do with the success one can achieve, are generally those who are too lazy and too afraid to work hard for their dreams. You clearly are not one of those people (ready to blame anyone or anything else), but are smart and want to get ahead or get even further ahead. You wouldn't have picked up this book otherwise.

Let's do a little exercise in three parts.

Step one: look at your current situation

- Where are you, both physically and mentally?

- Are you spending enough time with your kids, and are you able to give them all the things you want to be able to give them?

- Are you present for your kids, i.e. are you there in mind as well as body?

- What can you do to be more present with them?

- Are you thinking about all the things you aren't able to give them? That in itself is not a bad thing, but acknowledge it ("I'm not in a position to give them what I want to financially, with my time, with my attention – so I'd better start making some changes to improve my situation").

Step two: verbalise whatever it is you wish you could be

- "I wish I could live in a bigger house, in a better neighbourhood, drive a better car."

- "I wish I could afford to take the kids on that holiday."

- "I wish I could enjoy this trip rather than worrying about how I'm going to afford this lavish lunch they've just ordered."

- If you are a contractor/freelancer, "I wish I could take a day off and not worry about getting paid today."

Once you've acknowledged whatever you are worried about or have regrets about, then you can get to work on resolving it.

Step three: ask yourself, "What do I want?"

Be very specific here. So instead of saying, "I want more money", say, "I want to double/triple my current salary". Don't just say, "I want to spend more time with my kids", say, "I want to be able to spend an hour in the morning and a couple of hours in the evening with my family". When you have a clear and precise goal, you can then develop a clear and precise plan to achieve that goal.

Find out where you are today and where you want to be tomorrow. Now you have two points to plot on a graph:

i.   Your current situation – where you are today – and

ii. Where you want to be, i.e. your dream position.

With these two points in place, you can now start plotting your course, planning out how you are going to get all the things you want.

- I earn £50K.
- I work 60+ hours a week.
- I spend no time with my kids.
- I rent a two-bedroomed flat.
- I have three months' rent money in savings.
- At the end of the month, I have £200 surplus cash.

- I want to earn £80K.
- I want my average work week to be 40 hours.
- I want to spend an hour with my kids every evening.
- I want to buy a three-bedroomed house.
- I want to have one year's worth of mortgage payments in savings.
- At the end of the month, I want £1000 surplus cash.

Figure 1 Find out where you are and where you want to be.

Now decide how hard you are prepared to work, how much time you are prepared to spend and how many sacrifices you are willing to make in order to achieve your goal. If this sounds like a call to action, 5:00am starts and working harder than you ever have before, don't worry – it doesn't even have to be difficult in the slightest.

Remember I mentioned that your current life is a reflection of every decision you have ever made? Now take a moment to track back those decisions and see how they have lead you to where you are versus where you want to be. The truth is that to get to where you want to be may not require as much hard work and sacrifice as you initially think. In fact, just a series of small changes may do it.

You can start to make your way there by changing some of those decisions that have got you to where you are now. So instead of saying, "I choose to watch TV instead of going for a run", how about choosing to go for a run instead of watching TV? Changing your decisions will change your results. How about compromising and choosing to sometimes watch TV and sometimes going for a run?

ACTIONS	RESULTS
• I don't work out. • I don't put time aside for professional development. • I allow myself to get distracted. • I don't set goals.	• I'm not fit enough. • I'm not progressing at work. • I'm falling behind at work. • I'm not achieving anything.

Figure 2 Notice how none of the results are based on how hard you work, but only on the actions you choose.

You can apply this to any aspect of your life. Change the input and the output will automatically change itself, without you having to put in any more significant effort. The direction in which you travel is more important than the speed and intensity you put in. You can work really hard and make lots of sacrifices, but if you are heading in the wrong direction you will not arrive at your desired destination. Orient yourself towards your goal, so that any step you take towards it brings you one step closer.

Let's return now to spending time with your kids. We are going to try to balance this equation:

What is the least amount of time I need to trade to earn the maximum amount of money?

Financial services, you immediately think. Well it's true that bankers, stockbrokers and tax consultants do earn a lot of money and receive hefty bonuses. But although they earn much more money than a factory worker they don't have nearly as much free time, and certainly don't work from nine to five with an hour for lunch. Clearly there is a correlation between the amount of time and effort spent at work and the amount of financial reward gained. The graph is one that plateaus out, so it's your job to know where that plateau is, and then to decide what is the return or opportunity cost associated with this decision.

Earnings Over Time

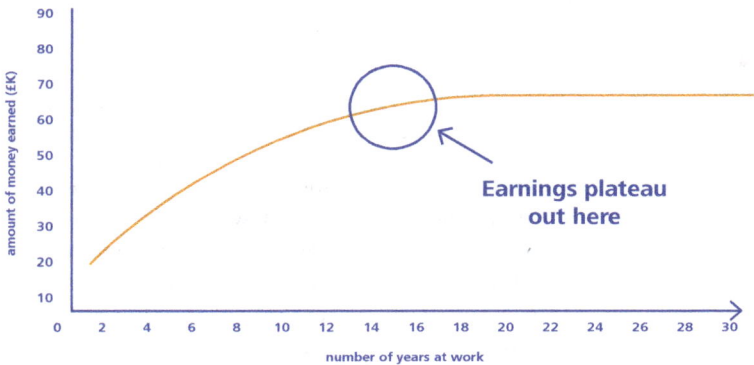

Figure 3 After a certain amount of time in the same job, earnings can plateau out.
Find this point and start learning new skills before earnings become stagnant.

Generally when someone is going to pay you a lot of money, they are going to take their pound of flesh in return. Ask yourself these questions:

- What skills do I have?

- What can I do quickly and well?

- How much are my skills worth?

In regards to the third point, you are worth a lot, no job can pay you what you are worth and will only pay what your skills are worth.

You may, for example, make the best cappuccino in the city; no one can make a cappuccino as well as you can and you win your friends' approval every time they come over for a dinner party. But how much is your cappuccino-making skill worth on the open market? You know how much it is worth.

Look at the people who are making serious money. They are not significantly better than you; in fact, they may not be better than you at all. They are certainly not working double or triple the amount of time that you are, or putting in that much extra effort, yet they are making double or triple the money that you are.

Why is this?

The answer lies in the skillset and specialist knowledge that they have. Note that this does not mean it's any better than your skillset or knowledge, it just means in today's economic climate, employers are willing to pay more for this skillset, in the same way that your current work-related skillset is worth more than your cappuccino-making skillset is.

Of course, the good news about skills and knowledge is that they can be learnt.

Search online job boards, and find out how much these jobs are paying. Are you earning above or below the average for the work you do? If you are earning below the average for the job you are currently doing, then you need to knock on your boss's door and ask why they are paying well below average for this position.

If you are not earning the maximum figure offered on that job board, find out why. Which skill gaps are missing, what experience do you need to gain and just who is this employer who is paying the maximum figure? Remember, that number is the greatest amount the market is willing to pay for your current set of skills. So ask yourself this: Is that maximum figure going to be enough for you to live the tomorrow that you visualised in step three above? If it is, that's great. And if it isn't, it is better to know now – this book will teach you some clear techniques for achieving this goal.

That's not to say that there won't be costs involved. There will be a cost to fill those skills and experience gaps and initially it will likely mean spending less time with your kids. But keep this mantra close to mind:

'Pain is temporary, success is permanent'
– Eric Thomas

Find out how much time it will take you to acquire these skills, and whether you can expedite the process. In almost all cases, the answer to the latter will be yes, you can speed up almost any process. Put down the newspaper and stop staring out of the train window on your commute to work. Choose to study on the train or at the station instead. If you drive, turn off the radio and get some audiobooks or podcasts; there are podcasts on every conceivable subject, find them! Spend some money on training – it'll get you to your goal quicker. Just using your lunch hours productively will gain you an extra five hours a week! When else are you going to find five hours a week just for yourself?

If that maximum figure on the job board does not hit the figure you need, then there are plenty of others out there that will. Read through the job specifications – they tell you precisely what they want – how much more of a clue do you need? Bridge those skills and experience gaps in exactly the same way as above. There is no pain involved in this. It's simply a matter of making different choices and decisions.

Time, much like the 119 bus, waits for no man. A minute will turn into an hour, an hour will turn into a day, a day into a month and a month into a year. There is nothing you or anyone else can do to stop time from passing. What you can do, however, is choose what you do with this time and where you want to be at the end of a given period. Do you want to attain that position and lifestyle or not? Remember that this is your choice and your future life is dependent upon what you choose now.

6

When you really have to do two things at once

Part of the way you are going to be able to get time for yourself to breathe is by getting more sh!t done and getting it done faster. There's certainly an element of multitasking that will help, but being judicious in choosing what to do, prioritising and calculating the opportunity costs involved is even more important.

Multitasking – doing it effectively

Multitasking, as we all know, is the ability to do several things at once and when done properly, enables you to get more done in less time. When done incorrectly or just for the sake of doing it, you won't actually accomplish anything. There are certain combinations of tasks that create an efficiency when done together (e.g. listening to a podcast whilst cooking dinner) and other tasks that are inefficient when done together (e.g. repairing a car engine while cooking dinner). Get the combination right and you'll burn through your to do list and have your evenings to yourself.

A simple example. You're home alone looking after the kids, the house is a total mess and you've got to get their dinner sorted. The youngsters finally fall asleep for their nap, and you now have exactly one hour to get all your jobs done. This is where your multitasking skills come into play. Your three tasks are:

- Cooking dinner
- Cleaning the house and

- Doing the laundry.

Done in order of importance, you'd probably go for the order listed above, taking you a total of an hour and a half. Since the children are only going to nap for an hour, you're not going to get it all done. Epic fail!

The concepts I want to present here are:

- Choosing the correct order to get all or most of the things done within the time allotted and

- Setting certain tasks in motion without finishing them, before moving onto other non-related tasks.

In this example, load the washing machine first and get that job started, so that before it's finished, you can get the food in the oven. And whilst the food is cooking, you can start cleaning the house. Whereas the washing machine and the oven can be left to go on their own, the vacuum cleaner can't.

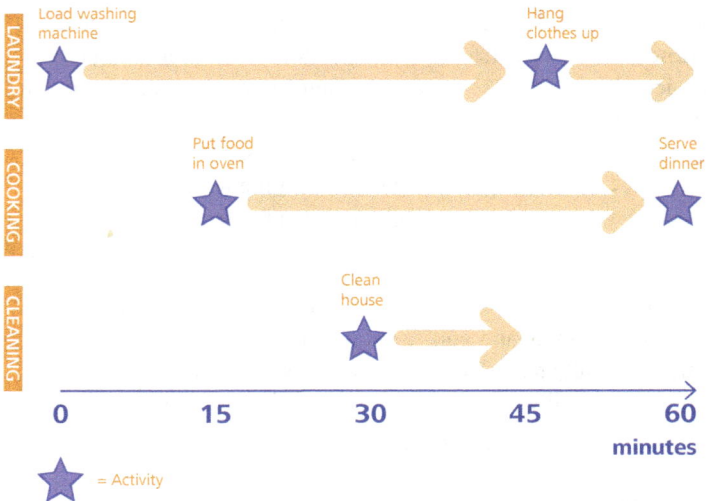

Figure 4 Doing tasks in parallel can get them done faster than when done in series

Identify which things you can set in motion and leave versus those which need your full attention to complete. To turn back to our domestic god case, by the time you'd have finished the vacuuming (which ironically would probably have woken the children up from their slumber), the washing machine could be unloaded and the food served, all tasks done in less than an hour, leaving you with some chill-out time before your little angels wake up fresh and full of energy. Now you can enjoy the afternoon with them, knowing that you've done your chores for the day. And when they do go to bed for the night, you'll have an evening free from any domestic responsibilities.

To take this one step further, if there are other people you need to work with, try to get them to work whilst you play. Schedule your tasks and dependencies around others. Send out emails and task lists just before your downtime begins, so that whilst you are playing, others are working and when you are ready to come back to work, all your dependencies are cleared.

Be judicious in what you choose to do – cyclic versus one-off tasks

Start being judicious in what you choose to do and evaluate the opportunity cost of everything. If in the same time as building a rocking horse, you could clean the house, do the shopping and file your paperwork, then evaluate whether building the rocking horse really outweighs all the other tasks. This decision-making process will help you get the maximum benefit from your time.

The rocking horse example also demonstrates the concept of singular versus cyclic events that will help you prioritise tasks more effectively. Building a rocking horse is a one-off event; it will happen once and when you have completed it, you won't have to do it again (until they break the rocking horse…). Tasks such as cleaning the house or washing the dishes, however, are cyclic tasks, insofar as no matter how thoroughly you clean the house or how well you wash the dishes, they are going to be dirty again, and you'll have to do the

27

task repeatedly. Building the rocking horse takes the task off your list completely, and you can always wash the dishes afterwards. If you put off building the rocking horse, that giant cardboard box will sit in your hallway for weeks to come.

Evaluate your tasks on a case-by-case basis and rank the items in terms of importance and urgency. Does building the rocking horse trump making dinner, for example?

Burning through your one-off tasks generally means clearing your to-do list and frees up time for yourself.

But remember that one-off tasks tend to take longer than cyclic ones, partly because we have built up speed and proficiency through repeated practice.

It's all about prioritising. Although there will be certain things that will need to take precedence over others (for example, changing a flat tyre if you're due to go on a bike ride), many tasks can be planned for in advance and you can make sure that you have mechanisms in place to automatically handle those without needing to be too heavily involved. Paying your bills is a good example of the advantages of the one-off versus the cyclic, where rather than wasting hours every month in physical or phone-line queues, you could simply set up an automated payment. Whilst it may take some time up front to change all your payments to this system (maybe even longer than paying the bills, which you're now very fast at), by the second or third time you should start to see that you get a return on your time, similar to the concept of return on investment. The things that will save you time further down the line may take up more time and effort up front.

Get your kids involved in the to-do list

As your kids grow, they will want to take part in the cleaning chores (at least, for a while!). This is because they don't see them as chores, but as play. Even though they might get in the way and turn a five-minute clean-up into three hours and a small mess into a gigantic one, by keeping cleaning fun they will want to help out and become better and faster at it. You shouldn't wait for them or go to bed to clean up. When they see you tidy up after them and when they join in with the process, they will understand that their toys don't put themselves away and the house doesn't magically clean itself.

Kids are very good at creating causal relationships and will correlate the state of the house directly with the mess they make and the time they spend joining in with the cleaning effort. Start this early before they rebel on you.

If I start something, does it mean I have to finish it?

Generally yes, but in practice when your baby wakes up unexpectedly from their nap, you are not going to be able to always finish whatever task you were part-way through. Don't stress, know that you had the right intention and was giving it a go. Things out of your control will take precedence. You can't control outside influences, so don't get hung up on them. Go and attend to your baby and finish the task later. Flexibility and adaptability are two important qualities that every dad needs.

In fact, leaving tasks unfinished can work to your advantage. Instead of rushing to finish a task, you can use the baby waking up unexpectedly as a forced break. Come back to the task later without the time constraints and you will end up doing a better job of it.

7

The rat race is going on without you

Whilst you are spending time with your kids, especially during the week, there will be the continuous hum whirring inside your mind telling you that the rat race is going on without you, and that whilst you're spending time with your children, others are out there making money and taking opportunities that you aren't. Although people speak more often of natural motherly instincts, there does exist a natural paternal instinct too, and even though modern, western society would sometimes have us believe that it doesn't exist, that feeling of wanting to provide more financially does still beat.

Whether you choose to quash this feeling or not, you may as well acknowledge this fact: There is a lot of money in the world and it is there for those who want to earn it. Generally speaking, those who work harder and longer will reap more rewards than those who don't. Determine where the point of diminishing returns kicks in and where the graph (see fig 3) of time versus earnings plateaus out.

When you assess these turning points, you'll be able to calculate just how much that extra time spent earning that amount of extra money is really costing you. The concept of diminishing returns was very simply and aptly explained to me once by one of my university lecturers. It went like this: Imagine an apple. With the first bite, you eat fifteen percent of the whole fruit. The same with the second and third bites. After that, you will start getting less apple per bite, even though you are putting more effort in. This is the notion of diminishing returns.

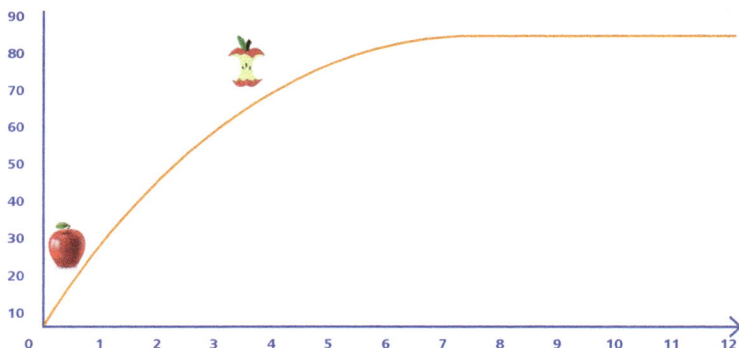

Figure 5 More than half the apple is eaten by about a third the way through the process. The rest is diminishing returns; when you hit this point it becomes better to focus your effort elsewhere.

Although you could work longer and harder, the returns on that time are diminishing and whilst on paper you are bringing in more money, in reality the extra costs on your family time will outweigh the residuals that you are making. This is something that you'll have to put a value on yourself.

Time isn't reversible and your babies aren't going to be babies forever. It may sound clichéd, but toddlers soon grow into pre-schoolers, who then become children and so on until their childhoods have gone. In our current society, childhood itself seems to be shrinking and children can have little time to just 'be children', indeed nowadays, childhood seems to be shrinking even more than job stability. There will be periods when additional work has to be done, of course, but like the conscientious father that you are, you are plotting your way to the top, with the idea that when you get there you will have more time to spend with your kids. It's a laudable plan, but unfortunately you aren't the first to conceive of such a thing. Bear in mind that:

i.   When you reach the top, you may well find yourself with less time and even more stress and

ii. By the time you do get an opportunity to spend time with your children, they may have grown up.

But it doesn't have to be all doom and gloom. Yes, the rat race will go on with or without you, but if you can't get out of work, then make that time up with your children elsewhere. Once the deadline has been met, make sure that you take a couple of days off. At the very least, take the weekend to make it up to your family. Whether it's a special treat, a trip to an amusement park or a day at the beach, try and make it something out of the ordinary. Explain that sometimes daddy has to work, and it's not that daddy prefers work than play but that sometimes it's essential. This will teach your child two things:

i. That money does not magically appear (although it can magically disappear) and

ii. That daddy is thinking about them and whatever daddy does or has to do is ultimately for their benefit.

Acknowledge that the gravy train is going around and that you need to get on it. This is, after all, your primary task as the breadwinner, especially if you are the sole breadwinner and your wife/ partner hasn't yet returned to work. If she does return to work, will the extra income she brings in outweigh the amount of money you can earn in overtime? If flexible working conditions exist, will it be worthwhile one of you working traditional working hours and the other doing evenings and weekends, i.e. earning money around the clock and alleviating childcare costs? Everyone's financial situation is different. Remember that it's not simply a case of how much money you earn, but boils down to expenditure versus income.

School play versus board meetings – can you be in two places at once?

One of the first jobs I had as a fresh-faced early twenty-something, was as a web designer/developer. It was the start of the dotcom boom period (post y2k apocalypse) and the company was set to launch several websites, having sold online advertising space for a lot of money (advertisers were paying big money for banner ads in those heady days). One of the lead developers on the database side – a nice, congenial chap, probably in his late thirties/early forties – was told in front of the whole office that he had to come in at the weekend to make sure the site went live smoothly. The developer in question said that it was his son's birthday and that the family had organised a big party and trip for him that weekend. This held no sway with the CEO, who was not afraid to threaten to fire him if he didn't come in.

This taught me a valuable lesson, twelve years before I would become a father myself, about work-life balance, and I vowed there and then never to be in that position myself. Of course, here is the rub: the higher you progress in any hierarchy, the more money you can expect, but with that comes the extra responsibility – the late nights, the weekends and the inevitable missing of your kid's parties, days out, school plays and so on.

I talked to one of the other designers who witnessed the event, a guy from Norway who told me the harsh realities of the utopian dream of becoming the big chief and not having to miss your child's birthday. His philosophy was that if you want a simple job where you start on time, finish on time and where nothing can go wrong, become a window cleaner. (He also told me that if you want anything done in an organisation, then to speak to the head and not the ass of a company – I may well be compiling a book of Norwegian sayings…) Of course, there are jobs where you can start and finish on time and never have to stay late or work weekends. Those jobs are acceptable – indeed, ideal – for some people, but by virtue of the fact that you are reading this book, you and I are the kind of people who 'want to have our cake and eat it'.

Is it possible for you to achieve your career ambitions and have a healthy work-life balance?

This is a subject I found myself becoming increasingly interested in. Several years after the developer situation above, I witnessed an example of almost the polar opposite. By now, I was working for one of the major VFX houses in London, on the fifth Harry Potter movie. One of the company directors was coming in at ten o'clock every morning (nothing surprising about that, as most people in VFX come in at ten) and leaving at three to pick his kids up (most VFX artists stay until seven or later). Another director was able to leave at four o'clock and work on his laptop on the way home. Of course, if any of us non-director types tried that, we'd be searching for alternative employment very soon.

That lifestyle is certainly attainable, but I don't imagine for a moment that either of those directors got to where they were by working six-hour days. There's a level of sacrifice and hard work that needs to be done upfront to reach that stage, and goodness knows how many birthday parties they missed to achieve the six-hour working day they now enjoy.

The examples above raise two points:

i. How can I work a six-hour work day and

ii. If I'm working six hours a day, surely it won't be long before others overtake me and I'll be pushed downwards instead of rising higher?

Let's start with the first point. You can accomplish a six-hour work day quite easily. In fact, nowadays you can achieve more in less time by working remotely than by going into an office with all the inefficiency that entails – commuting, settling in, endless cups of tea/coffee, constant breaks and chit-chat. I recently spoke with a producer who said that getting six hours of work out of an employee is a major achievement, and that typically they expect around four hours of productive work a day. If this is the case, is it any wonder jobs are going elsewhere?

Work less – earn more

I have worked from home myself on occasion and managed to plan the day out in a way that suited my own lifestyle and routines. Instead of waking up, getting ready, running for the train, being inevitably delayed, finally arriving at work and having my morning coffee, I instead woke up, turned on the laptop and started working straight away, before any of my work colleagues had even left the house and before either of my children had woken. By nine o'clock I had achieved the same amount of work that I would have achieved by two in the afternoon in the office. I then took my son to nursery, returned home and wrapped up any remaining work for the day before going to collect him at noon. Then we spent the whole afternoon together.

Sounds too good to be true?

Well yes, obviously you've got to get the work done and you have to be on call and be able to answer emails as and when they come in. And there might be some end-of-day administrative tasks to take up a chunk of your evening. But you'll find that when tasks start to impinge on your own time, you will be able to do them four or five times faster than in the office. Many jobs, especially IT-related tasks, can be done remotely; nowadays a VPN (Virtual Private Network) isn't needed and many forward-thinking companies are using cloud-based solutions. (In fact, I am writing this very book using a cloud storage system between Canada and the UK). Wherever my travels take me, I can use the cloud and work uninterrupted.

Forward-looking companies are the types of establishments in which you will thrive in as a dad. What is your company's approach to technology, remote working and time-saving tools that will allow you to do more in less time? If they are resistant to these changes (and there are few valid reasons they should be), it may be more of an uphill challenge to get more time for yourself, regardless of how efficient and ahead of the curve you may be. Generally, you will find middle managers are the ones most resistant to cloud-based solutions. They will cite security, confidentiality, NDAs etc. to block any kind of remote work setup. Of course, the real reason is that their jobs depend upon managing (controlling and micro-managing) staff, and if it is shown that staff can manage themselves, why would we need middle-managers at all?

The second point raised was the possibility of getting overtaken by others who are working longer hours than you. Let's take a look at how you can minimise the chances of this happening.

It's crucial to know how your company assesses its employees' contributions, whether it's by how many hours they spend in the office, how much they achieve or who is having drinks with the boss. If you are planning on working remotely or for fewer hours, make sure you have visibility. Make sure that everyone, especially the boss, knows what you are doing, that you have delivered and that you deliver ahead of schedule (working smarter generally delivers ahead of time). Having increased visibility will show you to be a top player and it will be harder for others to overtake you purely on the number of hours they spend in the office. If anything, this will separate you further from the pack when you show you have accomplished more in less time (but obviously don't tell them you've spent less time on it; imagine how that middle-manager would react!). Although you are going to be competing against younger, more energetic guys who don't have the same family pressures as you, your advanced knowledge, experience and motivation will trump their energy and long hours when you start to work smarter and are happy spending quality time with your kids.

Can you go to the school play at the same time as the conference call?

There will be times when no matter how important you are to a project, there will be diary clashes, maybe with a conference call overseas or a project going live at a precise time which has been defined months earlier. In this situation, you will have to make a choice and the pressures from work will be relentless. Regardless of how influential you are, you may sometimes have to put work ahead of your kid's major milestones; there is no getting around that.

This decision will depend upon where you are on your career curve, the importance of the meeting/business function, what you will gain from it and how significant the child's event is. There will never be another chance to attend your child's first school play, their first ballet performance or football game. These special moments won't come back, whereas there will always be important work meetings and events.

If you do decide to put a work function ahead of a child's event, then spend some time talking with your children, telling them what you do and why it's important. Helping them understand and keeping them involved in your day-to-day challenges will help them to anticipate that you won't always be able to watch their football game or their gymnastics trial. Make sure that the times when you are there for them, that you are there for them and that you give them your full, undivided attention. They need you to be there not just in body, but in spirit too. If you do have to miss their birthday party, then arrange a pre- or post-birthday treat for them.

8

Spare time – getting through your to-do list faster

We spoke earlier about getting though your chores list and how to multitask in order to get things done quicker. This section focuses on your own list, your real ambition list, the things you want to do and the things you enjoy. In the same way that having a wife/girlfriend does not make you oblivious to other women, being a dad does not mean that you suddenly give up on everything else you want. You had dreams before you became a dad which didn't involve your new station; if you don't make time for these things and pursue your dreams, you will lose your identity as an individual, and it will be difficult for you to give the best of yourself to your new family.

You've probably seen fathers whose goals and dreams have now deteriorated into whinges and whines of what could have been and what might have been. Sadly, they have become resigned to never achieving these goals purely based on the misconception of 'between work and the kids I have no time for myself'.

On the surface, it may indeed seem as though the to-do list has taken away all your time, but in reality you've actually gained more focus and increased productivity. When you were young, free and single you actually had a to-do list of chores as well, although it wasn't formalised and you probably weren't even aware of it. The fact is that things have to be done and we've now seen how to do them smarter and faster.

But what about the things that matter to you? How are you going to take time out to do the things that don't have much importance to your girlfriend? The answer is that you do them anyway; you don't need permission from anyone. Once you have accomplished the household and child-related chores, there's no reason not to go after your own goals. In fact, the only person holding you back from accomplishing them is yourself.

So put sleep aside and put relaxing and chilling out aside; there's plenty of time for all that after you've accomplished your goals. Yes, you might be tired, it might be difficult, but remember that 'pain is temporary, success is permanent'. In reality, it shouldn't be difficult or painful because this is something that you want to do.

Letting excuses get the better of you is not going to achieve what you want. Neither your kids nor your job are stopping you from achieving your goal – if they were, you would have reached it before you had a family. The fact is that we all put up our own obstacles. Now that you're a father, your reduced me-time actually gives you the perfect opportunity to go and achieve the things you want to, because when you feel that you have less time (the key word being 'feel'), you'll strive to make that free time really count.

Remember also that by doing something for yourself, you are a actually being a good dad and leading by example, teaching your kids to go for their dreams and not to accept or put obstacles in front of their dreams.

Waiting for an opportunity versus making an opportunity

This is important at any time of your life, but especially when you have children. Doing something is not always difficult. But finding the opportunity to do it can be more elusive. When you have the chance to do something, it's usually best to take the opportunity, even if you don't feel completely ready or in the right state of mind. There is never going to be a good time to do anything, and the stars are seldom going to align and give you the energy and inspiration to carry out your dreams. Instead, you must take opportunities when they come your way.

Planning your other tasks around these unexpected opportunities means that the household chores can wait, to some extent. If you have an opportunity to make big strides towards your goal, and towards something that could improve your life, then take that chance. If you don't, you will end up rueing the missed opportunity and furthermore ensuring that you are not in the right state of mind when the next opportunity presents itself. Take the opportunity – or better yet, make the opportunity – and you will feel so much better afterwards that you will forget about your tiredness and be able to give more back in return.

As we will discuss, there are ample opportunities to make time for yourself: the commute to work, your lunch hours, when the children nap or when they sleep. Get yourself in the right state of mind and energise yourself ready to make the most of these times.

9

Selective multitasking

Not everything can be done immediately, so it's vital to prioritise what is important to you and what does in reality need to be done right now. Balance out what's important short-term and long-term. By only addressing your short-term goals, you will find it difficult to make any real progress in life. Accomplishing short-term goals is akin to chasing your tail; remember that the majority of these goals are cyclical and no matter how much time you spend on them or how well you do them, you will be dong them again very shortly. That's not to say that you shouldn't do them at all, since these short-term goals are what keep life ticking over. But you need to make sure that you're not focusing on these only and failing to address your longer-term goals. Long-terms goals are those which will make real, measurable progress to your life. But both are important in their own ways, so do both – the short-term goals first so you can get them out of the way and then the tasks that will help you reach your long term goal.

Writing your book, gaining a professional accreditation or building your business idea generally won't take the twenty minutes that vacuuming the house will. Your long-term goals will take months or years to achieve and when you are progressing in steps of half an hour a day/week, you can begin to see how important every opportunity is. To use a cricket analogy, when chasing a big total, you're not going to hit every ball for sixes and fours. In fact, the majority of runs will come in singles. Keep picking off the singles, and when the chance comes to hit a four or six, then go for it. But don't turn down the singles.

I made a whole animated short film in just twenty minutes a day. Yes, it took fourteen months to do, but I wouldn't have accomplished it if I didn't take every opportunity that came my way and forged my own opportunities. You can't always wait for opportunities to come to you. Like any good forward (football) you are going to have to create time and space for yourself and not rely on your midfielders to serve you up a string of opportunities.

You are going to be a fulfilled dad when you find yourself not only raising your kids and providing them with everything they need, but simultaneously fulfilling your own dreams and ambitions. That's what separates you from being a good dad and a super-dad. Leading by example and showing your kids that they can achieve their dreams too is more powerful than lecturing and badgering them to work hard.

You can't help anyone else to breathe if you can't breathe yourself. Make time for yourself to breathe; put your oxygen mask on first before helping others.

10

Earning versus spending

Does spending money mean you will have a better time with your kids? Obviously a day out at an amusement park or play centre is going to be more fun than staying in watching TV. When you start adding in all the extras - two children's tickets, two adult tickets, lunch, snacks, parking – the bill is going to be quite high. And when your budget is already stretched, these costs are going to have you thinking more about how much everything is costing you and less about enjoying the day out. Yes, things do cost money, there is no getting away from it. And despite the fact that you might love your job, and hopefully find it fulfilling (bearing in mind that you spend more time there than anywhere else), the main point of going to work is to earn money.

There are two things to do with that money: save it or spend it.

In the next chapter, we'll look at various combinations of these two options, but this chapter is about when and where to spend your money. It's important to remember that spending money on your kids' enjoyment is a thoroughly worthwhile expenditure. So enjoy your day at the zoo, spend the extra money for the fridge magnet photos by the gorilla cage and spend those extra few pounds on purchasing the priority non-queuing tickets at the theme park. Why work so hard if you can't spend a few extra coins?

The great secret about money is that the more you spend, the more comes back to you. I won't go into the law of self-attraction – there are many excellent books on the subject (one of them being The Secret by Rhonda Byrne), but the essence of it is that when you spend freely you will earn freely. Whilst you're busy counting every penny instead of enjoying yourself, earning those pennies will become more of a struggle and less enjoyable. So don't worry about spending money on enjoying yourself with your kids; after all you are spending money on things that you don't want to spend it on, things like insurance, taxes, fees etc. over which you have no choice.

That is not to say you should throw your money away lavishly, so agree on your children having one toy each from the gift shop – the dinosaur or the puzzle, but not both. Set some boundaries and encourage your children to help choose what to buy. They will understand that there is a price associated with everything and that having more does not correspond with being happier.

Don't be too spendthrift. Many studies show that children value your time far more than your money, and your child won't know the difference between a high- and low-quality toy. Indeed, it's quite likely that they'll be more interested in the box it came in, before losing interest in both the box and the toy a few days later. So whether you treat them to a cheap and cheerful day out or an expensive, lavish one, for them it's the feeling of shared exploration and discovery that makes it exciting. Even though you know precisely where you are going, acting as though you are exploring and discovering with them will add to the excitement. Even when they figure it out as adults (did my dad really drive us around randomly and yet always happen to coincidentally find the most amazing beach?), these are the childhood memories they will cherish.

Spending money on your child shouldn't be thought of a way to buy their love or make up for the fact that you feel you've neglected them during the week – you haven't neglected them, you were at work and they are reaping the fruits of your labours. So spend when it's appropriate, particularly when you will gain something for that extra expenditure, like paying ten percent more to get better tickets at the theatre. This isn't about throwing money away or being miserly; it's just being smart with your money and teaching your children not only the cost of things but more importantly the value of them. Learning the value of things and that having more doesn't equate to being happier is an important lesson that they will take into their adult lives.

11

Saving versus spending

It is said that most arguments in a relationship are about money. If your wife hasn't gone back to work yet, chances are that you are earning all the money. Look at it from her point of view. She may have been working full-time, earning a good income and perhaps been financially independent before becoming a mother. Now all of a sudden she has a baby or babies and isn't able to work for a while. Perhaps she misses work and doesn't like being temporarily dependent upon you. By the same token, you are now temporarily earning all the money and since your hours are paying for everything, you might not like suddenly having to justify how you spend that money. Shouldn't you have a say in how the money you've earned is being spent?

Well the answer is yes, but as is often the case, theory and practice are not the same thing, and you are better off accepting this than trying to find the logic in it. Talk about your situation and your household expenditure. If you're not comfortable telling your girlfriend how much you earn, then don't; there's no reason to disclose that information. Even if you're in a marriage you need not feel compelled to disclose your wages. As long as you are openly discussing household expenses and agree on and work to a budget, you're going to know what you can spend money on. If the monthly income isn't going to stretch to something, this should be clear to both of you.

Being in debt

Whatever you do, don't hide debt from your partner. As we mentioned in the introduction, life today is not like in the seventies or eighties where a man was expected to keep his household ticking over on his own. Circumstances have changed and it doesn't make you any less of a man if you find yourself struggling to maintain the lifestyle you want. Playing it all macho in front of your partner whilst secretly struggling to make ends meet is not only ruinous for your relationship but ruinous for your health too. Debt can be seen as something of a necessary evil in our society, but managed correctly you can use even this to your advantage. If you are in a large amount of debt, it's essential to speak to your partner and seek some help.

Keeping up with the Joneses

No matter how modern we have become and how much we have evolved, we are still tied down to those primal instincts that dogged even the cavemen, and find it necessary to 'keep up with the Joneses'. Regardless of whether I write a sentence or a paragraph about how keeping up appearances is unimportant and how everyone's circumstances are different, you are still going to feel pressure from the guy who has more than you and whose kids have more than yours do. You are already smart enough to know that these material things don't matter, but what I'm going to speak to you about is how to deal with the times when the world (potentially including your partner) will make you feel a failure because you don't have a fast enough car, a big enough house or when your kids aren't going to as good a school as the next person.

If other people feel compelled to remind you how often they take their kids on nice holidays, well good for them. You too will take your children on executive, far-flung (expensive) holidays – maybe not just yet but it will come. Not only will you have a nice car like Mr Jones, but you'll have a better car than him. Just bide your time. Although you don't know their circumstances, chances are that they're not earning significantly more than you. If they've been helped along the way to get the things that they have, then take satisfaction that whatever you have, you've earned it. You didn't get any hand-outs from anyone to buy your car or house, but have made your money yourself and when you do buy a better car, it will be all from your own hard work.

Of course, your kids are growing up quickly and they will constantly see others with the latest toys and clothes. Marketers are smart and they know how to target children with gimmicks and advertising. Other children can be even smarter and know how to create a demand where there was none before and how to make other kids feel bad that they don't have the latest 'must have' item. As a good parent, you will have already explained the value of things and that having more doesn't mean being happier. But as your children are increasingly exposed to the outside world, the more they will receive messages that are in variance to the ones you've been teaching them.

After you've guided your children through this, there is still the issue of your partner. Whatever discussions (or arguments…) you have with her, you shouldn't at any point feel any less of a man because others have more than you do. If you need to work harder, then work harder. But do it because you want to progress yourself, not because you want catch up with Daddy Jones. Even when you do catch up with him, there's going to be Emily's dad who has bought her pony lessons.

How long are you going to keep up with everyone?

There always will be people with more than you and there will always be people eager to remind you about it. Of course, this is not a new phenomenon, fathers from the previous generation, remember those role models who kept the house ticking over on their own? Even they had these same pressures on them, and they too managed to keep these hidden from their children, in much the same way you are trying to shield your kids.

You can't afford to let the narrow thinking of others affect you. Whilst it's possible that some of them are looking out for you and trying to help, chasing others just to prove that you can keep up is self-defeating. Tell yourself that you will achieve everything and more, but that making yourself miserable, stressed and deflated is not the best way to achieve those goals.

12

When to save and when to spend

Open up a spreadsheet. In fact, download one from my website here http://www.workingparent.info/personal-cash-flow-forecast-tool. Enter how much you bring home after the government has robbed you and squandered away your money – I mean after you have paid tax (sorry, I live in England – I hope your governments don't incompetently waste as much money as ours do). Now enter all your household expenses in the next section. Add more rows in here if necessary; the spreadsheet will auto-update. Once you've finished, the spreadsheet will show you how much money you have left over.

Now you have a precise idea of how much money you have and how it is being spent. If you're happy with the cumulative total, then hotfoot it to a financial adviser, see where you can best invest it and start pencilling in dates for upgrading that car. If, on the other hand, it doesn't make for such pretty reading, it's better you know now. This kind of honest assessment with yourself is important, and better than the naysayers telling you. Now that you can see where you are and where you want to be, there are two strategies to improve that final figure: either you need to be earning more money or spending less.

Whilst the second option will have a faster turnaround, the first option will be the one that really improves your situation. Don't dwell on the fact the figure isn't what you would like it to be – the whole point of a forecast is that it is just that, a forecast. This tool gives you the exact methods of improving the figure and shows where improvements can be made. Whilst it's important to cut, make sure you cut out only the waste, the things that aren't necessary. Once you've done that, you'll be able to prioritise what's important and when doing those activities, you'll enjoy them even more because you've quantified the value they bring.

Living in such unstable times, it's important to put some money aside, and even if you are in permanent employment, your income is not immune to the general state of the economy. Putting money aside for longer-term goals will start taking the stress out of your life, so prioritise what's important and create mini pots in your savings plan for these. You will quickly realise which material things are genuinely important and hold real value. Financially, you will be better off and mentally you will know that you are building something solid for your children's future, assuring that they won't be wanting later on for the truly important things.

13

Permanent work versus contracting – how to make more money per hour

Another change from previous generations is the concept of a job for life, and there has been a huge increase in the amount of people choosing to work as contractors and freelancers rather than in permanent jobs (if such things as permanent jobs still exist). Being a contractor means you should be earning more than you would do as a permanent employee. Your permanent counterparts are being paid holiday pay, sick pay, pensions, health insurance etc., but you as a contractor are not. Make sure you know what the going rate is and appropriate the money you earn into some kind of savings. Especially important is putting money aside for pensions and for times when you are out of contract. Find an accountant and see if you can set yourself up as a limited company. There are many advantages in doing this, including tax savings, as not only can you claim allowable business expenses against your income, but if your partner is not working, you may add her as an employee of your company. Disclaimer: None of this constitutes any business or legal advice and the rules are different for every country – make sure you see a qualified accountant before you proceed. I cannot and do not guarantee these numbers work in your country/state and the rules are subject to constant change. Do not proceed until a qualified accountant has talked you through the process.

The way it works is that you can add a tax onto your day-rate – in the UK this is known as Value Added Tax (VAT) where you add (currently) 20% to what you invoice the client. You will, of course, have to give some of this money back (13% in the first year, 14% in subsequent years) to the Inland Revenue, but you will still make more on your day-rate. Have your accountant find out what the minimum wage is before you enter into income tax and add both yourself and your partner to the payroll of your limited company. Then deduct any allowable business expenses, things like hardware, limited travel and any training costs incurred. What is left is subject to corporation tax which (currently) is 20%, and after that, the remainder can be shared in dividends between yourself and your partner.

Here is a simple worked example to illustrate the above. Let's say that you make five thousand pounds per month and that the minimum wage allowed before income tax is twelve thousand pounds, i.e. one thousand pounds a month. I've factored in the VAT calculations to keep the example simple (disclaimer: I am not a tax advisor, so please seek the expertise of a tax advisor or accountant as rules vary from country to country and are subject to change). Your monthly tax calculation would look like this:

Monthly Tax Calculation			
	Project Tasks	**£**	**TOTAL (£)**
IN	Income	5,000.00	
	A: Total In	5,000.00	5,000.00
OUT	Wages - you	1,000.00	
	Wages - partner	1,000.00	
	Expenses	1,000.00	
	B: Total Out	3,000.00	3,000.00
PROFIT & TAX	C: Gross Profit (A-B)	2,000.00	2,000.00
	D: Corporation Tax (@20% of C)	400.00	400.00
	E: Net Profit (C-D)	1,600.00	1,600.00

Figure 6 Setting yourself up as a limited company helps you keep more of your money.

If you imagine that on £5000 a month you'd be looking at 40% tax, then you would have £3000 after income tax and before any further deductions. In comparison, as a limited company you would actually take home £4600 (i.e. the £5000 you made minus the £400 you paid for corporation tax). In this simple example, you are £1600 better off a month – all it will cost you is some time to visit an accountant to set it all up for you, and the cost of the accountant will be factored into expenses.

You will need to spend a bit of time each month collating your expenses, and your partner will need an on-going account for her national insurance payments. She may also be entitled to maternity pay from the government, if appropriate. If others try to make you feel guilty about your reduced tax bill (and remember that these are the same people who will remind you that they have a better car than you), ignore them; their claims simply aren't true. Remember that you are generating VAT for the government. This is money that didn't exist before and no permanent employee would have generated this extra money for the economy in the way that you just have and you are paying corporation tax at 20%.

14

Making quality time truly quality – how to switch off

You know that when you are spending quality time with your kids you should mentally switch off from all your work issues and financial woes. But in practice, how do you actually do that? Somewhere in your head, a voice will be telling you that a deadline is imminent, that the competition is getting ahead of you and that you could and should be moving forward in some way or another. Unfortunately, your inner voice tends to tell the truth at times you do not want to particularly hear it.

It's true that whilst you're spending time with your children, you could be getting ahead of or keeping up with the pack. But don't forget that this is true of any given time – it's not just the time you are spending with your kids but equally when you are at work that you could still be doing more.

Look at your daily routine and analyse your periods of downtime. No matter how hard you are working, there will be periods when you find yourself doing less. You may feel that time spent with your kids is downtime, but the findings from your analysis will show that there is already an abundant amount of time lost unnecessarily for you to cut out first. Knowing that you will have opportunities to work on your ambitions at other times during the week/day will allow you to relax and enjoy the time you are spending with your kids. Once the kids are asleep, it's time to get to work. Knowing that you will be working later on will help you to enjoy the free-spirited fun that you are having in the here and now.

But as well as asking yourself, "How much can I actually work?" there has to come a point when you must switch off. Yes, the issues and concerns you have will still be there, and the only way to solve them is by addressing them and working on them. But your problems will survive you taking a night off, and when you wake up the next morning you will be in a better state to solve them. Take a break when it is appropriate to do so. If you have achieved a major milestone, make sure you acknowledge it and give yourself credit for achieving it, and don't stress out if you are behind schedule – it could just be that the schedule was unrealistic anyway.

15

Travelling away for work

Travelling away for work and not being there for your children is quite a challenge when trying to build a strong bond with them. I should know – by the time my first son reached three, I had been away on work for almost a whole year and have been away for pretty much the whole of my second child's first five months. In parenting, as in life, learning how to juggle is an essential skill that you need to master.

In the current economic climate, you will need to grasp opportunities as and when they present themselves, which may mean travelling to faraway locations for work, whether you want to or not. Of course, you might actually choose to work away from home as your dream job isn't located close to you. Whilst the second scenario seems much easier, the choice involved can be harder, since it isn't borne out of necessity like the first option. Either way, you are likely to feel guilty about putting your ambition ahead of your family, as you take steps to becoming an industry heavyweight rather than a heavyweight super-dad.

Work is essential to everyone, modern super-dad or not, and it's no less important to you than it was to previous generations of fathers. After all, your efforts at work are what enable you and your family to have the lifestyle you want. Whether you choose to work away out of ambition or necessity, travelling away from your kids means that you are making a great sacrifice to give them that lifestyle.

Following your ambitions

When 'choosing' to work away from your family, there are some considerations to help you factor in the returns you will be hoping to gain:

How long will you be away from your kids?

- Are you making more money away than you would be if you stayed local?

- Will this job lead to better potential jobs closer to home?

- Are your children able to join you in your new location?

- Is the new location a better environment for them?

- What is the time difference and would you be able to talk to them regularly?

- Who is going to be their father figure whilst you are away?

Weigh up any benefit that you gain from following your career versus the price you will pay in not being there for your children. Although what you are doing is no doubt noble in many respects, remember that a) your children will not know (yet) that you are making a sacrifice for them and b) whilst you're not raising them, someone/something else is.

You should know that prolonged periods away from your kids will create a separation and a distance between you and them; they may come to see you as an uncle who visits occasionally instead of a dad who is always there.

By following your dream, you follow your natural course in life. By failing to follow this course, and instead taking any job just so you can stay close to home could lead you to:

i. Blame and resent your family for holding you back from your true dream and

ii. Achieve only a small amount of success in comparison to that gained by following your dream – do you really want to see your family as your jailers?

With the choices laid out for you, it is up to you to make the final decision. Think about whether you can relocate your family to your new work environment. Is the job you are taking a permanent move or is it a stepping-stone towards something better? Consider your children's ages. If they are still pre-school age, you have more freedom to move around, so should seriously consider following your passion and having your new family come along for the adventure. If you have older children and moving en masse would cause considerable upheaval, you will need to consider carefully just how much you want the job/career and weigh up the alternatives. Are you instead able to take a job more locally, which, whilst not doing exactly what you want to do, will give you a measure of stability, and allow you to pursue your goals outside of normal working hours?

Doing it out of necessity

When you are working away from home out of necessity, the decision is a lot easier, as the choice has essentially been taken away from you. The downside is that being away from your kids will be much harder to stomach than if you were away following your dream. If you are going away out of necessity, then remember that it is temporary, and that as soon as something better or closer to home comes along, you can take that opportunity.

If you make the decision to be away from your family, you need to consider who will be raising your children whilst you are away and how you can maximise quality time with them when you are there. Plan it out before you go.

16

Homework – how to switch off from work when spending time with your children

You spend upwards of forty hours a week at work, and if you are in a senior position you probably bring work home too. It is very easy to advise mentally switching off from work whilst spending time with your children, but in practice you may well be preoccupied with issues that need resolving and thinking about how you can work towards those solutions. It's also likely that you'll be thinking, directly or indirectly, about money.

To keep yourself fully engaged with your child, remember that those work issues will still be there when you get back into the office. Solving them now on your own at the weekend will only get you so far; the solution may require a team collaboration and on-site implementation. Even if you do send that e-mail, will it be actioned immediately? Are you going to sacrifice what little time you have with your kids to work on something that will not be actioned until Monday at the earliest?

Being there in body but not in mind with your child will grate on your nerves and have you clock-watching until nap-time, so that you can jump on your smart phone and speed-type that message you've spent the whole morning thinking about.

Don't do it. Instead, find something that you enjoy doing with your child. Remember that this is your time too – you've worked for the whole week and deserve to do something fun. What would you enjoy doing on a weekend morning or afternoon? Chances are if you enjoy a particular activity, then your child will enjoy it too. Of course there's a balance to be struck here. After all, a whole afternoon of playing video games and eating nachos sounds great, but setting your child on that route too early will see you never getting your hands on the game controller again!

17

When your partner doesn't have time for you

It is common to feel that your partner doesn't have enough time for you any longer and vice versa. It may be that:

i.   The primary caregiver doesn't have enough time for the breadwinner due to the after-effects of childbirth/looking after the children all day or

ii. The breadwinner doesn't have enough time for the primary caregiver due to excessive work pressures.

It can be either way around but since you have got this far into the book, we'll assume that you, the father, are the breadwinner and that the mother is the primary care-giver.

When she doesn't have time or energy for you

Whilst trying for a baby, your sex life was probably going through the roof, and chances are that you didn't miss any opportunity to 'try', even when you needed a night off. Once she became pregnant, you could be forgiven for thinking that she'd got what she wanted from you. As she became larger and closer to her due date, your role changed from midnight lover to midnight runner. And now the baby has been born, it seems like such a long time that you probably can't remember ever having actually been intimate with her at all.

Unfortunately, this is a path that is set to continue for a while longer. But although her body and hormones have gone through a huge change, your hormones have returned to normal. If anything, having been denied your natural urges for so long will have made you even hungrier for it.

So what can you do?

She is clearly not ready and as a caring partner, you don't want to appear selfish and inconsiderate towards her. Yet the fact remains that you still need satisfying.

And therein lies the great conundrum. You may be a parent now, but you are still a man and whilst your partner may not be able to give you what you want and need (yet), there will suddenly appear to be many other women who are able to give you just this. Note the key word 'appear'.

There is a reasonable amount of research to show that it is during this time that many extra-martial affairs begin, some studies suggesting that one in ten men cheat on their partners during pregnancy (see What's Your Pregnant Man Thinking? by Robert G. Rodriguez). We're not going to discuss the rights or wrongs of this here; that is a subject for another book. What we are going to talk about is getting through this period and getting you and your partner back to the loving, sensual relationship that first bought you together to conceive a child.

In the past, she may have been impressed with many things about you – it could have been your looks, your personality, even your paycheque, but whatever it was, there was definitely something that drew her to you and you to her. Those things that initially attracted her to you are not the things she needs right now (unless it was your paycheque, in which case do not lose your job!). That is not to say that she will never need or want those things again – she will, but just not right now. 'Now' could mean several weeks, several months or even a year or so. She needs something different from you at the moment – support, understanding and not you constantly badgering her for sex or bemoaning the breakdown of your sex life. And there are more productive times to bring the subject up than when she's feeding the baby at midnight!

Remember that your partner's energy levels will be at an all-time low. If she is breastfeeding and the baby is in the same room as you, chances are that both of your sleep patterns are disrupted, so you have two cranky people – one exhausted at having to look after a baby and one stressed out with work pressures. Both of you are frustrated in different ways and ready to blame one another as the cause of their angst. Repair the situation before you start looking for sex.

Start looking for solutions

There is a lot you can do now to help the relationship. You may feel that you are not receiving the appreciation and credit you think you deserve, and it's reasonably likely that your efforts may go largely unnoticed. There will be some correlation (albeit not directly) between the extra effort you put in around the house and the improvement in your relationship. So do more than your fair share and take on her problems and concerns without expecting her to take on yours. Don't worry – this is a temporary engagement and you will get your time in the sun again. Getting the woman whom you love back to her rightful self will see your relationship rocket to the next level.

At the weekends, take the baby from her and do everything you can from feeding and changing nappies to taking the baby out of the house on your own. This will have a dual benefit as you will be spending quality time with the baby and your partner will have some time for herself – something that she's had precious little of. Of course, it's important to balance this with spending time with her and together as a family, but don't underestimate the importance of her having her own time and space. After all, just as you were your own person before you became a parent, so was she; she needs her time, space and identity back just as much as you do.

Verbal tennis

Often, we don't use our mouths and ears in the proportions in which they were given to us. Listening is an art, whereas talking is a competition. When either of you are talking, it is really important that the other one listens. The caricature of us men is that we try to find quick-fire fixes to problems and that of women is that they want to speak and express themselves without necessarily looking for solutions. Whether these Martian and Venusian traits actually exist or not, one thing that is very important is to let the other person finish and not to turn the conversation into a competition. Neither of you needs to outdo the other, there is no prize for proving you are more tired than your partner, or more stressed, or that you have the least amount of time to yourself. Don't get into the destructive pattern of interrupting or volleying a response immediately back at each another, but instead learn to listen.

There are many excellent books on the art of listening. The first chapter of What Every Parent Should Know About Raising Children by Dr Roger McIntire is an excellent resource for learning to listen and communicate effectively.

18

When you don't have time for your partner

There is an inverse situation to your partner not having enough time for you and that is when you do not have enough time for your partner. Since this book is primarily aimed at those dads/breadwinners who are already extremely busy, who do not have an hour-long lunch break and who never leave the office at five, it is likely that you are already stretched by all the demands placed upon you.

Much time and effort has been spent to reach the heights that you are at or are imminently about to attain. In many cases you are, even if only subconsciously, taking work home with you. If you are unfortunate enough to have a smart phone or tablet, then work will follow you right up to the moment you close your eyes (Hint: Turn off your Wi-Fi and mobile data unless you want work to impinge upon your REM time.)

A driving force behind many successful people is competition and the need to constantly be outperforming others. As I mentioned earlier, you were once that star in the office that the older, married guys and fathers looked at with derision. But now it's your turn to feel the pressure from those highly charged, energetic variants of your younger self.

There are, of course, only twenty four hours in the day. So by the time you take out the hours for sleep, work and commuting, how much time are you left with? If you are a lucky dad, you will have six hours left, but it's more likely that you are looking at three or four. Now factor in some time with your children. How much do you have left now? What about when you cram in everything else that you have to do just to function – eating, bathroom time, cooking, cleaning and so on? Is there much time to spend with your partner? Is there any time to spend on yourself?

Clearly something has got to give way. Yes, you need to work and sometimes it'll be late and at weekends. Work is your primary income, after all (more on secondary and passive incomes later).

If you commute using public transport, then use this time to do more than stare out of the window or read the newspaper (newspapers are only ever filled with bad news and advertising anyway – you can spend your time better). Be judicious with your time and use it for yourself, to do all those things that you are thinking you should be doing when you are at home spending time with your child. For instance, I am typing this book whilst on the train to work. My train journey is twenty-five minutes. Fifty minutes' return a day, five days a week makes two hundred and fifty minutes a week. When else are you likely to get over four hours to yourself during the week?

Factoring in your lunch hours in a similar way could give you up to another five hours a week. Combined with your travelling time, you could find yourself around ten hours a week (Monday to Friday) – even short journeys and waiting for buses, trains and tubes/subways all add up. Plan out your commuting time in the same way as your work tasks and schedule in jobs that logically link together to burn through the to-do list (take that annoying paperwork on the train). When you start seeing results and progress towards your goals, the happier and more content you will be in the evenings, knowing that you can focus solely on family time. Bear in mind that your partner is unlikely to have those same ten hours to herself, so you can give her some of your time and attention, content that you have given enough to work for the day.

Having now allocated time for yourself, you can use some of your evening to give to your children and to your partner.

19

When you don't have time for yourself

If there genuinely is no downtime, the commute is too short or impractical to work in, your lunch hours are always spent catching up on work and every night and weekend is spent in the office, then you need to re-evaluate. Are you really making enough money to forego any kind of healthy work/life balance? If you are making that much money, then do you have a plan for when you can start to scale back? How much money would you need to lock away to start investing time in your family and in yourself?

Running the tank down to empty is going to mean burnout. I know you won't think it'll happen to you, that you can handle the pressure and that you know what you're doing. But ask yourself this: How long can the tank run on empty for? And if you were to refill before you got to empty, wouldn't you have more energy and be hugely more efficient in whatever sparse time you have?

Whatever your financial goals are, plan things out and insert breaks for yourself – burning yourself out racing to the finish line is actually more inefficient then including timed breaks where you can come back with double the amount of energy. Measure the gains against the trade-offs and make sure your partner understands these too. If you can attain financial freedom sooner, then you will be able to enjoy an enhanced quality of life, but what quality of life will this be if your kids hardly know you and your partner is distanced and accustomed to being without you?

Though your ambition is noble, in reality you are backing yourself into a corner. Whether it's for a weekend or just a day off, come out of that corner and plan something really special with the children so they know that when daddy is off work, it is going to be a fun day and that they have your full attention. Spend whatever time you can spare talking with your children, even if it is just a few minutes in the morning before rushing off to work. Never underestimate how valuable these precious minutes are; your children know that you are busy but will appreciate the fact that you are taking time out for them. It will keep the relationship going if you specifically ask about things that are important to them, and don't rant at them at how busy and overrun you are.

Make time and space for yourself

All the best sportsmen make time and space for themselves and manage to make things look easy. Give yourself a chance to listen to music, watch a movie or football game or whatever it was that you did before you became so busy. Share your interests with your children too. They will have more fun with you when you are happy than when you are going through the motions and there are few things more satisfying than watching your favourite sports team with your child beside you (you'll have to let them know which team you are (both) supporting, of course!).

20

Falling out of love – it only takes a minute

Falling in love is a wonderful thing it is. Sometimes it happens in a single minute, and sometimes it's a longer, slow-burning experience, but however long it takes, it is always magical and you are consciously aware of it the whole time. Falling out of love can also happen over any time frame, but is something that you may find yourself unaware of until you are so far down the road that turning back is either too cumbersome, difficult or plain undesirable.

The reasons for couples falling out of love are wide and varied, but neglect through not having enough time for one another need not be one. Whether adjusting to first-time parenting or struggling to cope with multiple children, the pressures on both parents today can be quite overwhelming. Try to examine the pressures you're facing, whether it's the difficulty of finding enough time to spend together, or the effort to 'keep up with the Joneses'.

If you do start to feel that your relationship is drifting away, try to understand that it is never going to be the same relationship as it was in the early, happy days (I am assuming that your early days were happy days as neither of you ought to be entering into or persisting at a relationship that was not happy at the very start).

An important concept to understand here is that your relationship has moved onwards; that is to say that it has moved forwards.

Moving a relationship forwards is a good thing. After all, if you'd never moved your relationship forwards, you'd have never got past saying "Hello" to her in the first place. But now your stations in life have changed; she has become a mother and you have become a father. Your relationship has moved from two younger, single people having fun into a relationship between two parents with responsibilities.

Remember the reasons why you came together in the first place and understand that this would have happened regardless of which woman you were with – sorry to burst your bubble, but it may have been no different had it been that beautiful lady sitting across the train from you. So have your little fantasy about how your life would be better with this random beautiful lady or even an ex-girlfriend if you must, but then wake up and get back to business.

Be the leader here and work on your relationship. Although some people will tell you to be realistic, I say quite the opposite. You are the driver of your relationship, don't think that anyone else can make your life better and don't expect your partner to make you happy or improve the relationship. Instead, you take on that role. You be the one who makes that relationship work and you be the one who puts and keeps the magic in the relationship. You know what you want, so make it happen.

Another point of note is that as well as there being little or no time for one another, you may experience little or no energy or even worse, little or no enthusiasm for one another. You will both feel continually drained, from work and looking after children and though you still have other dreams and ambitions, all your conversation will now revolve around your new family. These conversations, if not checked, could easily turn into arguments over various aspects of raising children. If this becomes the case, realise that it's not because you and your partner are falling out of love, but because you are struggling to cope with the pressures of everything. Very few things in life can prepare you for the overhaul that having children will bring. A lot of these feelings are derived from the situation, and not from the fact that you and your partner are no longer getting on.

One of the best things you can do to keep your relationship sweet is to get the children into a routine.

Knowing that they will be going to bed on time will give you both the breathing space that you desperately need.

But don't use that time to argue. Remember that conversation is made up of listening and is not a verbal tennis match. Just being able to talk to one another will keep your relationship healthy and flag up any potential issues to act upon before they are too far entrenched to be resolved.

21

Seismic shifts – when continents move apart

Going away on business for extended periods will present a new set of challenges for the whole family unit. Your partner will be left to her own resources without you there to give her a break in the evenings, mornings or weekends. Your children will wonder where you have gone and depending upon how long you are away for and how old they are, they may not even remember you.

You, on the other hand, have complete and utter freedom! Your evenings are yours again. Your weekends are your own again and you can do whatever you please. You certainly won't be able to rush back home quickly and depending upon the time difference, it maybe even be too late or too early to phone them when you get back from work.

However long or often you are away from home for, it is worth planning out your time as:

i.   The business trip is not going to last forever and

ii. When you do get back home, you will want to make up for any lost time away from your family.

Use your evenings judiciously and take the opportunity to do things you wouldn't ordinarily do at home. This will prevent you from feeling homesick and will give you the chance to live your own life for a while, which in turn means that you will have more to give when you return to your kids.

While you are off enjoying your sojourn, you will need to consider how your partner is coping on her own. Struggling to keep the house and children in order and carry the responsibility on her own, she will probably not want to hear about all the fun you are having in the evenings and weekends, even if you did go to your first NFL game (keep that news to tell your friends!). Keep the conversation focused on her and the children when you do talk.

Make sure you speak as often as is practical. Depending upon where you are based, the time difference may make it impractical to speak during the weekdays but on the weekends do make time to talk to your children. This need not be an expensive option – using one of the numerous web chat messenger apps means that you can make free calls back home, and also has the advantage of allowing your children to see you on the monitor/phone/tablet; you don't want them forgetting you. They will understand that you are still there for them and indirectly will know that you are travelling away for work for their benefit, so that they can have all the things they need.

You will also need to consider who is playing dad to your kids whilst you are away? Is there someone to do all the things that you would normally do with them? Whether it is reading, painting or taking them to sports practice, will someone else be there for those jobs? This is especially important when it comes to the tasks that you normally do relating to their education. If you are the one who usually teaches your kids their letters or numbers, who is going to do this in your place? If no one does this, then you may be in for a surprise to learn that in your absence, they have forgotten how to count to twenty, something that you spent months diligently teaching them. Use your messenger apps to recap all the lessons that you would normally teach them on a regular basis. There's no reason why you can't teach them their alphabet and numbers over the phone and web cam. I managed to teach my two-year old boy to count to ten and twenty over the phone whilst I was away working on The Pirates movie.

22

Difference in standards

The biggest causes of contention between you and your partner that will occur in raising your child are when you both have different standards and expectations for your child's upbringing. Of course, this is not something that you would have known about before becoming parents and is very difficult to predict. Whether your standards are higher than your partner's or hers are higher than yours, you will be presented with particular challenges.

Before we progress, I am using the term 'higher' as there is no other suitable adjective to use. It is more useful to regard standards as 'all operating on parallel planes but widely spread and diverse'. That will obviously break the flow of the sentences, so I am using the term 'higher' to represent those standards that will promote more positive and empowering outcomes.

The issue of standards may well relate back to your own relationship when you first started living together.

Remember that period when everything was different and you took time to bed into each other's living habits? Well that time is about to reoccur and it may provide a clue as to whose standards and expectations for child rearing are higher. Of course, the difference here is that when a baby is involved, decisions have to be made, actions have to be taken and nothing can be deferred or allowed to slide.

In much the same way as the higher wage earner goes out to work, logic dictates that whoever has the higher standards (i.e. the ones that will promote positive and empowering outcomes) will ultimately take the lead in the decision-making process for your child's upbringing.

There is also an emotional stake involved now that will override any kind of logic and rationality. Both you and your partner have memories from your own childhood about the way in which your parents raised you. Try not to let these conflicting approaches to raising your own child become a competition over which of you had the better upbringing and ultimately whose parents did a better job.

Be objective when it comes to this. Do you really want to raise your kids the same way you were raised?

If the answer is yes, then figure out what the best elements of your upbringing were. Although they may have been suitable for that situation, is it still applicable to your child's situation today? Isolate the elements that worked and then separate yourself from it and approach it objectively. You will soon find a common theme and identify which values are important in a child's upbringing.

When your standards are higher than hers

Firstly let us assume that your standards are higher than your partner's. In this situation, you may experience feelings of anger and frustration because:

   i.   She will be spending most of her time with the child, so whilst you can teach and bring them up in the way you like when you are at home, you do not know whether all those principles and techniques that you hold in such high regard are being applied when you are away. You are going to feel frustration when none of your ideals are followed up by the child's mother during the weekdays when you are away working.

  ii. You are constantly having to redo or correct things that are not up to your standards. This will ultimately lead to bitterness as you spend your weekends not just talking about what you want to do, but actually practising what you preach. You try to be a good partner by leading by example and your partner sees that you do this. But by Monday mid-morning, all the effort and work you have done will be undone and standards will slip back. Imagine repeating this for months and years. Where is that going to take your relationship?

The problem with having the higher standards is that you feel as if you are the bad guy, that you are being obtuse and making everyone's life difficult, when in reality, all you want to do is to give your child the best upbringing that you can.

Rest assured that you are not the bad guy. But neither is she the bad gal. The fact remains that no two people have the same standards, but many of the challenges in parenting relate to how parents work together to bridge the gap.

Explain to your partner why you think certain principles and techniques are important. Avoid making any reference to either of your upbringings to avoid pride taking over from logic, or arrogance (from the partner with higher standards) and stubbornness (from the partner with the lower standards) taking over from rationality.

It is not a case of you telling her what to do, but more a case of explaining to her why you think these things are important. Be patient; the person with the higher standards also has the burden of responsibility as the standard bearer. Live to those principles yourself, avoid being a 'good talker', but ensure that you lead by example. Whether you perceive it or not, children learn from actions, and whatever they see you doing, they will want to do themselves.

When her standards are higher than yours

When her standards are higher than yours, you will face a different set of challenges and experience a different range of feelings on the emotional spectrum. Feelings of anxiety, inadequacy, low self-esteem and regret may dominate your thoughts.

Use this as an opportunity to reach your higher self and become all those things that you know you are capable of being. Try to understand that it's nothing personal and do not take any comments as an attack of your character – this is about putting the child's welfare ahead of any ego.

In truth, if your partner has higher standards than yourself it is actually a good thing. This is because:

- Initially the child will be spending more time with mummy than with daddy, so will be getting a better standard of teaching and

- You can learn from your partner – become a sponge and soak up whatever pearls of wisdom will be dispensed, regardless of how they are delivered. This is your chance to grow, grasp it with both hands.

Either way, never make it personal and always explain or listen to the rationale behind the action; ultimately you both want the best upbringing for your child. As this is so important, it is worth considering what the best approach actually is. Maybe neither of you has the right answer. This is a good opportunity to research and source information from experts. Either of you burying your head in the sand will not accomplish anything and we now live in a society where we can access information at the click of a mouse or a swipe of the screen. Use these resources to raise both your standards accordingly.

23

When you want different things out of life for your kids

This section is not about who has 'higher' standards, but is instead concerned with the direction your life is heading in. Again, this is not something you can predict upfront, but having children does change people. You both go from lovers to parents. When you were lovers, there was one dominant direction you were heading in; in fact you may have noticed little else. But now that you are a dad, your eyes are open to everything around you. This is not necessarily a sign of age, but more that your awareness levels are heightened when you become a parent. All manner of things will be drawn into sharper focus, from road safety to the community you live in. You'll start to question whether those things that were okay for you are good enough for your offspring. You may be surprised by the answer. But there is a reason why dads are the way there are – it is not by accident, but you too are experiencing a metamorphism and will have an image in your mind of how you want your ideal life to be.

The issue, of course, with having an ideal image in your mind is that your partner's image may be totally different to yours.

Does compromise always work?

Not really, no! Take the seemingly simple example of naming a child and the potential for disagreement here. Let's say you already have an ideal name for your child – Wilbur. You've had this name in mind for a long time and imagined the day that you and little Wilbur would go on days out fishing and camping.

However, your wife also has a name in mind, and it isn't Wilbur – she wants to name him Horace.

People, mainly those without children, will advise you to compromise. Okay, you could compromise, on a name that neither of you like – but where will that get you? You will have a child with a name that is your fourth choice and her fifth choice. In this situation, it is better to go one way or another, so that at least one of you is happy. Here, sacrifice is better than compromise – trade something to gain something else.

Extending this further, perhaps you want to live at the beach, but she wants to live in the mountains. Should you compromise half-way again and live in the city? Of course not – neither of you even want to live in the city! By always meeting half-way, neither you nor your partner will gain anything and both your lives will become a medley of half-hearted decisions for the sake of keeping the peace.

There is no simple answer to resolving disagreements, as the complexity and the infinite directions your lives could take is beyond any collection of books, but you need to find an approach that works for you. To find the principles and values that are most important to you, dig below the surface and superficiality of what you want.

An alternative solution to compromising on every decision and falling into this half-way house situation is to use a give-and-take method. In the trivial example above, say you agree to name the child with the name your wife prefers and you agree to live where you like – she gets the name she wants and you get to live where you want.

It is unrealistic to get everything your own way. Recall your young, free, single days – did you get everything you wanted out of life then? Did you even know what you wanted?

What you wanted when you were age five changed by the time you were age ten. By the time you were twenty, you wanted different things to what you had wanted as a fifteen-year old. Keep that in mind when you are at loggerheads with your partner over what you want now, because five years down the line, you may want something different. She too will want different things as time progresses.

Keep the dialogue open and always say what you want and make her aware of it. By expressing it verbally, she will come to understand you better (and help you achieve it), and its true value will become clear as you will either become very excited as you speak about it or the energy will fizzle out if it is not something you are really passionate about.

24

Secondary and passive incomes

Whilst we are well on our way to becoming a more progressive and equal society (lol), you as a father will still have natural instincts to play the hunter-gatherer role. It doesn't even matter if she earns more money than you do – you are still a man and your ego will hurt when you see other people earning more money and giving their kids more than you are currently giving yours. (Note: I didn't say more than 'you are able to' give your kids – your ability to give to your kids is unlimited.)

In previous sections, we've examined how to do better at your job and progress in your chosen career. But what happens after you leave the office in the evening, when you log out of your machine and when you mark out of your time tracker? Think of your ability to make money as water flowing through a tap. It doesn't make sense to turn that tap off. When you leave the office you are essentially turning off the tap.

There is an important distinction to make between 'earning' money and 'making' money. By going to work, you are earning money and you will be paid whatever your daily/hourly rate is. You can increase the amount of money you earn through overtime, promotion and bonuses but essentially the amount you earn is linked to how much you put in. Even more than that, there may be some ceiling that the company will cap your wages at.

Herein comes the principle of 'making' money. Making money is not capped by the time you put in. You can make money whether you are asleep or awake – it is simply a matter of setting up some structures that can create a long-term, passive income.

Passive incomes can be broken down further than this, into investments and long-form incomes. This is not a finance handbook (nor am I a financial advisor, find a financial advisor who can guide you through the right investment vehicle for your needs), but I will go over the basic principle of cumulative growth and diversified funds here. These two principles should set up an expectation of how you can use your money to create more money.

Cumulative growth is a very simple concept, but one that is not fully understood by many. Imagine that you invested £100 in year one, and it grew by 10% every year. Your annual growth table would look something like this:

Year	Value
1	100
2	110
3	121
4	133
5	146
6	161
7	177
8	195
9	214
10	236

Figure 7 Compound ten percent growth over ten years.

You can see from this simple example that in ten years you have more than doubled the initial amount of money you have put in. You may think that you don't have enough money to invest or money to put aside, but when you consider that the money which you put aside is working for you whilst you sleep, you can see why it can become quite a priority.

Rich dad, poor dad, somewhere-in-between dad

There is a story of three people who all earn the same amount of money doing the same job. One of them is poor, one is rich and the other is in between. How did this happen, after all they all earn exactly the same amount of money?

The answer is in how they chose to spend their money. The poor person spends all his money on 'stuff' or 'things'. You go to his house and you can't move for all the objects on the floor and the table-tops are full of possessions that the person has spent his money on. These items depreciate massively and have little or no resale value. Ironically enough, this 'poor' person probably has a better car than the person in the middle.

The person in the middle has spent his money on what he perceives to be assets, such as his house. He believes that he has made a shrewd investment, and perhaps he has in the long run, but a huge portion of his income is going to be spent paying interest on a mortgage back to his bank, maybe interest worth even more than the house itself. The next stream of his income will be spent on household bills and expenses – horrible things like buildings and contents' insurance. These are things which he will likely never need, but are a prerequisite from the bank to lend him the money. If he thinks these insurances are worthwhile, he will be in for a surprise the day he has to make a claim on them. Whatever money he has left over, he can choose what to do with it. Although he may decide to buy material possessions, ironically he won't have as much money to buy them as the 'poor' person does.

The rich person, however, spends his money on true 'assets'. Assets are things that will make him more money. He buys investments, ISAs, funds, stocks and shares. And with the money he makes from them, he buys more assets. You can see from the example above how much one hundred pounds can grow at ten percent, but that example was based on the assumption that you never put another penny into the fund. Imagine now that you add to that fund the money you earn from your day job. You are essentially doubling the value every year, which then cumulatively expands to make a lot more money. Certainly a lot more money than buying 'things' and 'stuff' will achieve.

Even though society doesn't like this truth, there is a reason rich people are rich, why poor people are poor and why a great deal of us are stuck in between. Shifting your spending patterns towards buying things that will make you money will reap dividends sooner than you think.

Two common reasons people make for not investing are:

i.   Not having enough disposable income to invest and

ii. Not knowing where or how to invest.

These are not insurmountable obstacles; in fact, they are not even obstacles at all. Firstly, what is it you are spending your money on that you are unable to invest it? What could possibly be so important that it takes priority over doubling your money? Of course you have to put food on the table and there may be hospital or medical bills to consider, but after that you have to examine your own priorities.

The second 'obstacle' is an even lazier excuse than the first. We live in the age of the internet, so it's never been easier to find out how to invest. There are independent financial advisors out there who will do it for you, many of whom won't even charge a fee, but take a percentage of whatever they make for you. If someone is going to make you twenty percent, let them have one, two or even three percent of whatever they make for you – it's a no-brainer!

Long-form money

Long-form money is gaining an 'income' from something that you sell, either physically or over the internet. Typically it will be in the form of some kind of IP (Intellectual Property) that you can monetise over time.

Long-form income is quite different from investments. With an investment, you place your earned money into an investment vehicle and let it grow. Long-form income does not require you to put in any money, but does need you to put in time to make a product. This book, for instance, is an example of long-form income; it took me many years of writing, rewriting and marketing to be able to create the book in the form of a saleable asset. Now that it's released, it only requires me to follow up on marketing the book.

Other examples of long-form income could be other multimedia products, such as mobile apps, e-courses (videos or printed) or webinars – if there is something you are passionate about, chances are that other people are too, and that you will be able to find a community which shares your passion. If you are also an expert in the field, then you will be able to turn that community into an audience. Perhaps you're an expert in finance or architecture or maybe you're an airline pilot or an astronaut. Whatever you are, you are sure to be good at it and there will be people who will want to learn from you.

There are, of course, some costs of producing the materials that you want to sell, but essentially the internet will allow you to work within a set budget. As little as ten years ago, creating and selling a multimedia product would be a near-impossible target to achieve, and there would have been numerous obstacles in your path. Back then, you would have to find a printer or video recording and editing facility – today you can purchase apps for under £3 to edit on your tablet. To run a marketing campaign would have meant booking out TV, radio and magazine advertising space and pasting your advertisement on the sides of buses and city billboards – today you can freely use social media to target the exact audience who will buy your product. If you are a keen fisherman, you can find with one hundred percent certainty internet communities where other keen fishermen frequent and talk to them directly through social media and forums.

The major factor to consider when pursuing a long-form income is the time it takes to invest and the unpredictable level of income you will receive. If you do decide to pursue this make sure:

- It is something that you are passionate about and

- That there is an audience for it.

Creating a product may initially be a few months of work, but then factor in another few months for the editing process and a few more for the review process before beginning on the design work required. Then allow for several weeks of market research before creating and executing a marketing strategy. As you can see, the few months of initial work that you were excited about will turn into a year or so of labour to launch the product.

Opportunity costs

So what is the opportunity cost of this? Opportunity cost is the cost of foregoing the next best option; that could be another project, gaining a professional qualification or rather importantly, spending time with your kids. As a busy dad, you may be already struggling to balance your work and home life, so consider carefully the opportunity costs of adding in another project. And if you do decide to go ahead, make absolutely sure it's something you are passionate about. There is no guarantee of the extent that you will be able to monetise it, but if you care about it enough then it will be a release, rather than a chore. To learn more about this subject, I recommend the excellent book Crush It by Gary Vaynerchuck.

Getting to the top – being a good role model for your kids

So we come to the perennial question of how to balance family life with career. Your quest to reach your goals may see you spend extended time away from your new family and there will be times when you tire of the rat race. We are about to enter into a period of increased competition, where balance of power is shifting between continents. This means that whilst some economies are going to be struggling and shrinking, others will be thriving and growing. You are going to face a global challenge for your job, one that is unprecedented in history. The old measures of being successful will soon become the standard for survival. So you can see how important it is that you are successful in your career (I avoid using the word 'job', as a job is something that ends at 5 or 6pm).

Being successful in your career is also the best way to set a good example to your children. Avoid being one of those fathers who constantly tells his children what to do, but instead 'be' what you want your children to aspire to become. When your children see how successful you are, they will learn from our work ethic. When they see the things that your money can buy and how happy you are, they will want to work hard at school to achieve the same things that you have.

Setting a good example will show your children how to be successful, but don't fall into the trap of thinking that is enough. Yes, it is great that you are being a good role model, but when you do have free time, make sure that it is spent first and foremost with your children. Find out about them, talk about things they are enthusiastic about and be sure to act upon this by doing things together that they enjoy. Try to spend time with them alone, go on days out, organise baby and daddy time where just the two (or however many children you have) of you do fun things together that you both like. Set a good example for them both as working dad and as home dad.

26

So what is really important – money or family?

The answer is, of course, your family, but your family needs money to survive and thrive. The golden ratio for this to happen is actually having enough money and time to spend with them. Until you can create a substantial passive income, you are going to have to trade your time for money. When you have optimised this trade-off, then you can start to balance your work and home. If you are not earning enough money for your family to thrive, you need to ask yourself why other dads are working longer and harder. Set yourself the target that you want to reach. How much money do you need to earn to be comfortable and happy? What are you currently earning and how can you increase it? How much time are you spending to earn that money? When you get the answers to these questions, you can start to optimise and figure out your work/life balance.

Don't fool yourself into thinking that you can find a healthy work/life balance when you are not earning enough money to keep your household going. This will just lead you from bill to bill, struggling to keep up. Instead, do the analysis. This will show you where you are and allow you to form a plan showing where you want to be and how to get there. Costs may have increased in recent years, but opportunities have grown even faster. Today, you can learn any skillset you want in a matter of hours. Whereas in the past you would have had to sign up for a course over several weeks or evenings, now resources on any subject are readily and freely available. I have learnt in-depth web analytics, internet marketing, book publishing and business analysis as well as new VFX skills all from the internet. Many of these are videos and seminars were on YouTube, ebooks were often only a couple of pounds and I had the content in under a minute. If your current job has plateaued, then skill yourself up for a new one.

There are many couples where both the partners are working and sending their children to day-care. But of course day-care has a cost. If you are fortunate, you will both earn enough to cover that cost, but if not, then you will need to weigh up whether it is financially viable for the lower wage-earner to go to work or take on the day-care responsibility.

A wise man once taught me that when a man has his financial situation sorted out, then he can do whatever he wants. For now, make that your priority and carry out a SWOT (Strengths, Weakness, Opportunities, Threats) analysis on yourself. You will soon see that only a few minor adjustments are needed to get to where you need to be financially. Once you are there, you can move on with the things that really matter to you.

27

Be a good father secret

I had initially titled this section, 'Be a good father secret – be a good husband/partner', but being a good husband or partner is really a by-product of the real secret.

To be a good father is to be good to yourself.

If you are good to yourself, you will be a good father, a good husband/partner, a good brother, a good son, a good uncle and so on. You can't expect others to treat you with the respect and love you deserve unless you treat yourself with that level of love and respect.

You are going to be a fulfilled dad when you can say that as well as raising your kids and providing them everything they need, that you are fulfilling your own dreams and ambitions. Leading by example and showing your children that they can achieve their dreams too is more powerful than lecturing and badgering them to work hard.

Whilst travelling around the world searching for work so I could provide for my family, I saw many in-flight safety announcements. They all made the same point about the oxygen masks. Being brave fathers means that in an emergency, we would all look out for our children first, but if we ourselves cannot breathe, how would we be able to help anyone else?

I hope this book has helped you in some way, but even if there is only one lesson that you take away from it, let it be that you can't help anyone else to breathe if you can't breathe yourself. Make time for yourself and breathe. Put the oxygen mask on first before helping others.

Here is another image from the same in flight safety card, which in part inspired me to write this book.

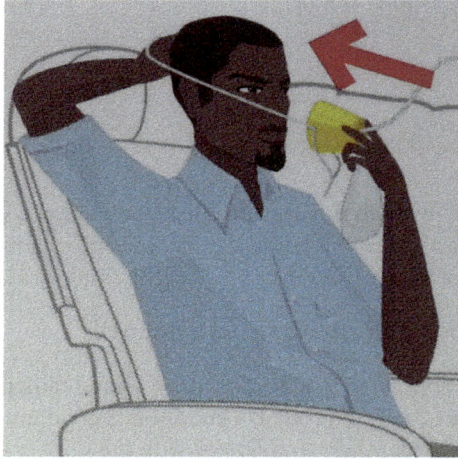

One last dedication before we finish (I know that some people skip the thanks section, so I wanted to put the most important one at the end). This whole book is dedicated to you, the dad. Being a dad is the most important and worthwhile thing a man can do, and goodness knows, society needs dads now more than ever. Take some time out to acknowledge what a great job you do and make time for yourself too.

Finally, please make some time for yourself too, it's really important both for yourself and for your child. Your children will grow up happier when you are also happy.

Thanks for reading, best wishes.

Farhan

Bibliography

'What Every Parent Should Know About Raising Children' by Dr. Roger McIntire (Summit Crossroads Press, 2012)

'The Secret' by Rhonda Byrne (Simon & Schuster UK, 2008)

'Crush It' by Gary Vaynerchuk (Vook, 2010)

'What's Your Pregnant Man Thinking?' by Robert G. Rodriguez (Authorhouse, 2005)

Please take some time to leave positive feedback on the Amazon store you purchased from and join our community at www.workingparent.info where you'll find many like-minded parents with whom you can share your stories. The site contains many resources, videos and content developed specifically for and by working parents like yourself.

If you want to learn more about the VFX work I do please visit my VFX and film blog at www.digitopiafilm.com

You can find my bestselling book, VFX and CG Survival Guide for Producers and Filmmakers here

Kindle - http://www.amazon.com/kindle/dp/B00BDV8GY2/

Paperback - http://www.amazon.com/Survival-Guide-Producers-Filmmakers-Guides/dp/1484021541/

Sincere thanks for reading.

Farhan